SOME KINGS AND QUEENS

R. J. Unstead believes that kings and queens must always seem larger than life. He portrays not only their royalty but also many other aspects of these people: their goodness and strength developing from weakness and confusion, and their shortcomings submerging their fine or lovable qualities.
R. J. Unstead's imaginative writing and William Stobbs' powerful illustrations add to the fascination of the lives of men and women whose slightest whim made history.

3 cde

Also by R. J. Unstead

THE STORY OF BRITAIN: BEFORE THE NORMAN CONQUEST
THE STORY OF BRITAIN: IN THE MIDDLE AGES
THE STORY OF BRITAIN: IN TUDOR AND STUART TIMES
THE STORY OF BRITAIN: FROM WILLIAM OF ORANGE TO WORLD WAR II

and published by Carousel Books

R. J. UNSTEAD

SOME KINGS AND QUEENS

Illustrated by William Stobbs

Carousel Editor: Anne Wood

TRANSWORLD PUBLISHERS LTD
A National General Company

SOME KINGS AND QUEENS

A CAROUSEL BOOK 0 552 54010 2

Originally published in Great Britain
by Odhams Books Ltd.

PRINTING HISTORY
Odhams Books edition published 1962
Carousel edition published 1971
Carousel edition reprinted 1972

Carousel Books are published by Transworld
Publishers Ltd.,
Cavendish House, 57–59 Uxbridge Road,
Ealing, London, W.5

Made and printed in Great Britain by
Cox & Wyman Ltd., London, Reading and Fakenham

NOTE: The Australian price appearing on the back cover in the recommended retail price

CONTENTS

FOREWORD

Kings and queens can hardly avoid being interesting. They stand apart from ordinary people, being more powerful, more generous, foolish or cruel than the rest of mankind. And there was always something mysterious about kingship. Even those who won their thrones through treachery or conquest usually claimed that the crown was a gift from God, for then men would give them reverence and obedience that they would give to no one else. Even in failure, a fallen king or a betrayed queen seems more pitiful than other humans.

In these stories, I have chosen kings and queens from various countries and periods of history; they were not all great rulers and many of them, to be truthful, were rather unpleasant characters. But all of them were interesting. All of them, because they were monarchs, were larger than life, and all of them made their mark on history.

R.J.U.

ALEXANDER THE GREAT

'LOOK! Look at the King's new horse! What a splendid creature! See how he kicks. No-one will ever stay on his back!'

The cries of the excited boys could be heard across the dusty parade-ground where, in the presence of the King and his attendants, half a dozen grooms were trying to subdue a magnificent horse that reared and plunged with terrifying strength.

One of the boys, fair-haired and taller than the rest, suddenly ran across to the leader of the struggling grooms and spoke to him sharply,

'Give me the rope, Amyntas. I will ride him!'

The startled man let go the bridle and before even the King himself could act, the boy had turned the horse's head and had led him away from the noisy crowd of onlookers. Patting the horse's neck with his free hand, speaking to him softly and, above all, making sure that the animal could no longer see his own shadow which had been the cause of his terrified behaviour, the boy quickly brought the horse under control. Then he leapt upon his back and rode across to where the King was watching from the shade of the cypress trees.

The King, no longer anxious, roared with laughter.

'Keep him, he is yours!' he shouted. 'You conquered him so easily, you must ride him to conquer kingdoms!'

The boy was Alexander, son of King Philip of Macedonia, who ruled a half-civilized kingdom to the north of Greece more than three hundred years before the birth of Christ. The horse was Bucephalus, the 'bull-headed one', and he was soon to carry the boy in triumph across the known world.

King Philip was a mighty ruler. By skill and cunning, he had made his little kingdom powerful, for he had not only subdued the lands that lay northwards, but he had made all the city-states of Greece, except Sparta, recognize him as their overlord.

Alexander was brought up in a draughty palace that echoed with the quarrels between his father and his furious-tempered mother, Olympias, but the lad was given an education to fit him for greatness.

He was taught how to ride, hunt and fight like any young noble but his father also summoned from Greece the great scholar Aristotle to act as tutor. From Aristotle, Alexander learned about science and mathematics; he grew to love Greek ideas and, above all, the stories of the Greek heroes who had fought at Troy. He knew Homer's long poem, 'The Iliad', by heart and he carried the book with him wherever he went.

Alexander was certain that he was more than a Macedonian. His father had the head of Heracles (Hercules) stamped on his coins, so the boy felt sure that he was descended from that legendary figure, half-god, half-man, and, on his mother's side, from Achilles, the hero of the Siege of Troy.

At 16, Alexander was left in charge of the kingdom while his father was on campaign. At 18, he commanded a wing of the army that defeated the Greeks and made them obey Philip. But soon afterwards, the family quarrels grew worse and Alexander and his mother had to take refuge in an uncle's kingdom.

Just when it seemed as if Alexander would never inherit his father's throne, for Philip had taken a second wife and had a baby son, he suddenly became King of Macedonia.

Philip was stabbed to death at a marriage feast by a discontented noble and, in the confusion, Alexander seized his chance with the speed for which he was soon to be famous. He won over the army with fiery promises, crushed the Greek cities that had jeered at the idea of taking orders from a mere boy of 20, and announced that he would raise a force of Greeks and Macedonians to conquer the mighty Persians whose empire stretched from the Mediterranean to the frontiers of India.

In 334 B.C., Alexander left Greece with an army of 30,000 foot-soldiers and 5,000 horsemen. It was a small force to challenge the numberless hordes of Persia, but although the archers and the cavalry were splendidly trained, the strength lay in the Macedonian way of fighting under their brilliant commander. The soldiers formed up in dense squares armed with pikes of enormous length, so that an attacker could not pierce the wall of spears; when the square, known as the 'phalanx', charged, no army in the world could stand against it.

Having prayed to his heroic ancestors at the site of ancient Troy, Alexander advanced to meet the army sent against him by Darius III, ruler of the Persian empire. He found the enemy drawn up on the far bank of a river. The Greeks hesitated, but Alexander plunged into the water with reckless bravery calling them to follow. The white plume was slashed from his helmet, his pike broke and he had just seized another, when he

was narrowly saved from death by his friend Clitus. After a furious battle, the Persians broke and fled.

Alexander sent some of the captured gold vessels and rare Persian cloth to his mother. To Athens, in honour of the goddess Athene, he sent 300 Persian shields with these words engraved upon them,

Alexander and the Greeks (except the Spartans)
won these from the barbarians of Asia.

With furious energy, Alexander now marched through Asia Minor, capturing city after city, but Darius himself soon advanced with an enormous army to put an end to this upstart conqueror. So confident was

In the distance the enemy were massed and ready

Darius that he brought his family with him, living in the camp in silk-lined tents with luxuries and slaves.

Again, the Greeks were victorious and Darius fled, leaving behind immense treasure and his wife, mother and young children who cowered trembling in the tent, awaiting the fate of royal captives. But Alexander treated them nobly.

'I am not here to fight against women,' he said. 'And my contest with Darius is not undertaken out of hatred. I have come to master the empire of Asia.'

But when Darius sent a letter asking for peace and friendship between equals, Alexander was scornful to the man who had run away. 'I have defeated your generals and now yourself,' he wrote back. 'Come without fear and you shall receive back your mother and wife and anything else you please. But do not write to me as an equal, address me as Lord of Asia and of all that belongs to you.'

The conqueror turned south. Syria was taken, Tyre was captured, Jerusalem was entered to the songs of the welcoming priests and then the great land of Egypt was reached. Here, Alexander founded a city at the mouth of the Nile and named it, like many others, Alexandria, in his own honour.

From Egypt, the Greeks marched back into Persia to fight Darius for the third and last time. His army was said to number a million men but it was routed and Darius fled once more. Eventually he was slain by his own bodyguard who hoped that Alexander would reward them, but he put them to death for their treachery.

The hard-bitten Greek and Macedonian soldiers now entered the cities of Persia behind their god-like leader. The treasures of Babylon and Susa filled them with amazed greed, but Persepolis, the capital, was more magnificent still. After a great feast, Alexander himself set fire to the beautiful city and utterly destroyed its temples and avenues of statues. He did this to show that Persia had been laid low, though he was afterwards sorry for the deed.

The truth was that the character of Alexander was changing. The noble youth was becoming suspicious and cruel. He still loved knowledge; he was as generous and brave as ever, but he began to behave like an Eastern tyrant, surrounding himself with slaves and Asiatic attendants, making even his generals bow themselves to the ground when they approached him. He had his trustiest old general put to death and, in a fit of temper, he stabbed his friend Clitus who had once saved his life.

Alexander soon became bored with all the feasting and athletic games that followed his victory. He told his soldiers to destroy their plunder, for he would lead them to fresh triumphs. Mounted on Bucephalus, he led them eastwards, conquering every tribe and kingdom that stood in his path until he reached the foothills of India.

The invincible army broke into the Punjab and defeated King Porus with his immense force of cavalry and elephants, for even these great creatures could not daunt the men who followed Alexander. As usual, he treated his foe generously and, leaving Porus to rule for him, he planned to go to the end of the world where, the Greeks believed, he would find the uncrossable river called Ocean.

First, however, Bucephalus, the marvellous horse who had died from old age, had to be given a splendid burial at a place where a city was to be built in his honour. Then a greater sorrow came to Alexander. His troops refused to march. He pleaded and threatened, but in vain. The men would not go on. 'I have known defeat only from my own soldiers!' cried Alexander when he gave the order to turn westwards.

On the way back, the soldiers suffered terrible hardships; half the army died of thirst in a desert but the survivors struggled on to Babylon. Here, Alexander set up a sumptuous Court and busied himself with endless plans for his vast empire which he would bind together by means of the Greek language and Greek culture. He was planning cities, harbours and voyages of exploration when he caught a fever in the marshes of the River Euphrates. He was still only thirty-two when he died at Babylon.

Near the end, his Macedonian veterans, eager to see their beloved leader once more, broke into the Palace and filed past the couch of the dying man.

'There will be splendid Games at my funeral,' he joked as they came slowly by, and then, almost to himself,

'It is sweet to have lived with courage and after death to leave behind immortal fame.'

MORE ABOUT ALEXANDER

Alexander the Great (356–323 B.C.) was the son of Philip II of Macedon, a soldier-king who trained his army so skilfully that, by 338 B.C., he had subdued the city-states of Greece. Jealousy and the long war between Athens and Sparta had weakened Greece since the Golden Age of Pericles, Rome was still a struggling little town fighting for its life against the local tribes and the great empires of the past, Egypt, Babylon and Assyria, had fallen under the rule of Persia.

Alexander was only 20 when he crossed into Asia Minor with an army of Macedonians and Greeks but his brilliance as a general and the discipline of his troops enabled him to defeat the vast Persian armies at the battles of Granicus, Issus and Arbela (331 B.C.). Leaving Macedonian governors to rule the conquered territories and the new towns which he founded, Alexander pushed into the wild regions south of the Caspian Sea, defeated the tribes, overcame an army revolt and married Roxana, daughter of a chieftain. The successful invasion of India was an incredible feat by a small army consisting mostly of foot-soldiers armed with pikes, bows and swords.

Though he was vain and cruel, Alexander was far more than a mere conqueror. His brilliant mind planned to unite his conquests into one great family of Greek-speaking people with Babylon as their capital. No-one can tell what the course of history might have been if he had lived longer; as it was, his empire was divided into separate kingdoms and most of them, 300 years later, became provinces of Rome.

ALFRED THE GREAT

A SMALL boy, wearing a scarlet cloak fastened by a gold brooch, glanced eagerly about him at the tall buildings, the archways and fallen pillars; 'Look, father,' he cried, 'across the river; there lies the palace of the Pope.'

His father nodded, patting the boy's head, as he turned to speak to the thanes and monks in his company. A couple of porters carrying wine-jars, paused for a moment. 'Foreigners,' said one. 'Franks or Saxons, I dare say, by their cloaks and fair beards.'

The year was 855, and the boy was Alfred, youngest son of Ethelwulf, King of Wessex, who was visiting Rome, where he presented His Holiness the Pope with splendid gifts wrought with the skill for which Saxon craftsmen were famous. Wessex was the strongest of the English kingdoms, and the Pope looked with favour upon Ethelwulf because he had recently won a stirring victory over the heathen Northmen.

Alfred and his father stayed a year in Rome and the boy never forgot the great city with its churches and stone walls. Its paved streets and air of learning were so different from his native land of woods and chalk hills, with little towns of wooden-walled houses surrounded by earth banks.

Back home again, Alfred's brothers saw to it that he was taught to ride and to use weapons like every nobleman's son but they soon realized that the sharp inquisitive boy was going to be the cleverest one of the family. There was a story that his mother gave him a beautiful book because he learnt to read it before his older brothers. Whether or not this was true, Alfred said afterwards that his boyhood lessons were all too few, with so much moving about during the troubles that came upon the kingdom.

His father found that the Northmen, who were also called Vikings or Danes or simply 'the heathen host', were raiding again. They came across the North Sea in their dragon-ships, made up the rivers and went ashore to fan out over the countryside. Far and wide, they ranged on stolen horses, to plunder and kill with such terrible ferocity that the people prayed nightly, 'From the fury of the Northmen, Good Lord, deliver us'.

King Ethelwulf died when Alfred was nine and soon it seemed as if a curse lay on the royal house of Wessex. The eldest son died within two years and the next son, Ethelbert, only five or six years later. Ethelred, the third brother, became king with seventeen-year-old Alfred as his devoted helper, but men shook their heads gloomily, for the boy suffered from a strange illness that brought bouts of sickness and pain. However, his spirit was so courageous that he refused to be ill when every fighting man of Wessex had to stand ready to meet the enemy.

One winter's day, a messenger from Mercia rode into Ethelred's camp and asked to be taken to the king:

'What tidings from my sister's husband, messenger?' asked Ethelred.

'Evil news, sire. The host has taken York with great

slaughter. The king of Northumbria is slain with his bishops and the kingdom is lost.'

Worse followed, for the Danes overran East Anglia and spread into Mercia, where they set up their winter quarters at Nottingham, building a stronghold near the river from which they could raid the country as they pleased.

The King of Mercia asked Ethelred for help, so the Wessex 'fyrd' or army marched to Nottingham where Alfred had his first glimpse of the terrible Northmen, with their horned helmets, mailshirts and huge battle-axes. By this time, the Mercians were too frightened to attack the enemy camp, saying that no-one had ever captured a Danish stronghold, so they gave them gold to go away, and the men of Wessex returned to their homes.

Naturally, the Danes came back, and Mercia fell. Wessex, the last Christian kingdom in Britain, seemed to be doomed.

In 871, when Alfred fought in nine battles, Wessex was attacked by land and sea. Raiding parties harried the south coast, but the main assault came down the ridge of hills to the Thames. At Reading, Ethelred and Alfred led an attack against the Danish stockade, but they quickly learned what the Mercians had feared, for, as a monk wrote,

> *'the heathens fought with valour, and rushing out of all the gates like wolves, joined battle with all their might. Alas! the Christians at last turned their backs and the heathen gained the victory.'*

The Wessex army retreated, but when fresh troops came up to join them, Ethelred made a stand at Ashdown. After a feast of triumph, the Danes followed and took up a position on a hill opposite. Confident that they would wait to be attacked, Ethelred went into his tent for Holy Mass. Suddenly, the Danes charged and Alfred was forced to take command. 'Fighting like a wild boar,' as his friend Bishop Asser wrote, he led a counter-charge with such skill that, for once, the enemy was defeated and forced to retreat.

The Northmen soon came back; Ethelred died and Alfred was hurriedly elected king by the Witan. He was only twenty-two and his kingdom was collapsing around him. By the end of the year, his men were so exhausted that he had to scrape together all the gold in his Treasury to buy a breathing-space from the enemy. Both sides were glad of the truce, for the Danes were settling in Northumbria and Mercia, while Alfred had to work desperately to rebuild his army, and to bring some order to his suffering people.

Four or five years passed before the Danes were ready to swallow Wessex. Under an able leader, Guthrum, their main army drove into Dorset, while another force prepared to strike from the West and a large fleet appeared off the coast. Exeter was captured, but Alfred hung on stubbornly at the enemy's heels until a great storm wrecked more than a hundred longships and drowned thousands of Vikings who were closing in for the kill. Trapped in Exeter, without supplies or reinforcements, Guthrum had to make a truce and retreat to Gloucester.

It was Christmas time and the people of Wessex drew a sigh of relief, for the enemy would not march again until the spring, since, in winter, the land was too flooded and short of food to support armies. But Guthrum was no ordinary leader. On Twelfth Night, when the season of feasting was at its height, he pounced on Chippenham, stockaded his main army and sent his

They fought the Danes

savage horsemen to ravage the countryside. Caught off guard, Wessex collapsed. The army was scattered, many thanes fled and Alfred was forced to take refuge in the swamps of Somerset with his family and household bodyguard.

Despite the old tale of the fugitive king being scolded by a peasant woman for burning the cakes, Alfred was not alone. Saxons came to join him in the reedy wastes of Sedgemoor until he had a force that could threaten Guthrum's flank. On a patch of higher ground, he built the Athelney fort, from which raiding parties went out

vith bitter courage

to harass the enemy, while messengers threaded their way across the marshland with secret plans to rally the men of Wiltshire, Dorset and Hampshire.

By Whitsuntide, the fighting-men of Wessex were trudging across the hills to meet at Egbert's Stone, high up on the downs, and when thousands had gathered there, with their spears and cooking-pots, their sons and rough-coated horses, a shout went up,

'The King! The King! Alfred comes with the men of Somerset!'

Cheers of unspeakable joy burst out at the sight of

their own king moving amongst them again with the calm assurance of a true leader.

Without delay, the Wessex army marched. They found the Danish host on the chalk slopes of Wiltshire above Eddington, where, locking their shields together, they tore upon the foe with the fury of men who remembered their savaged homes and slaughtered children. The Danes broke and made for their stronghold at Chippenham, but Alfred allowed no pause for victory feasts. Following hard, his men cut down the stragglers, captured vast amounts of booty and shut Guthrum in his fortress. Two weeks later, 'terrified by hunger and cold', the Danes surrendered.

When custom cried out for revenge, Alfred showed noble generosity. He fed his enemies and spared their lives. Awed by this spirit of true Christianity, Guthrum gave up his heathen gods and was baptized into the Christian faith, while agreeing to withdraw all the Danes behind a line drawn roughly from London to Chester.

Although this victory and the Peace of Wedmore allowed Alfred to rebuild his devastated kingdom, the Danes did not suddenly become law-abiding. Even Guthrum had to be given another sharp lesson and fresh bands of raiders had constantly to be driven off. The Danes of East Anglia were particularly troublesome, so Alfred captured London and brought Mercia under his control.

First and foremost, Wessex had to be made safe; the defenders must never again be caught napping. Alfred therefore organized the army so that some fighting-men remained on service whilst others tended the fields and afterwards took their turn in the ranks. To prevent the Danes from sweeping across a defenceless land, the King ordered his thanes to fortify towns with ditches, earthworks and palisades. Meanwhile, he sent abroad for shipwrights to help build a fleet big enough and swift enough to defeat the sea-wolves before they could set foot ashore.

But Alfred's true greatness lay in peace. His country was ruined, its churches and monasteries gutted by fire, its homes and schools destroyed. Trade had ceased, the people were hungry and lawless, the nobles too ignorant to know what to do. Alfred himself said: 'Hardly a man in my kingdom can read his prayer-book – or write a letter. I would have you set all the boys now in England to learning.'

He set a matchless example. Not only did he take a hand in the actual work of building churches and towns, but he designed houses, worked alongside craftsmen, founded schools and compelled even the nobles and eldermen to take lessons.

'It was a strange sight,' wrote a bishop of the time, 'to see eldermen and officials, ignorant from boyhood, learning with difficulty to read.'

The best pupils learned Latin, the language of educated people everywhere, but there were few English books for the others to read, so Alfred himself polished up what Latin he remembered from boyhood. Then he translated parts of the Bible, books on history and geography and Bede's famous History.

Everything interested this amazing man. He never wasted a minute, but divided up the day into periods for business, study, prayer, building and translating.

He was always on the move in the kingdom, distributing justice and visiting the twenty-five towns he founded or rebuilt. Yet he found time to have the old Saxon laws gathered together, with some new ones, to provide a written Code of Law. He encouraged trade and loved to talk to merchants and sea-captains to find out about strange lands, astronomy and new ideas. He kept in touch with Rome, brought scholars and teachers from abroad, cared for the orphans and the homeless, and taught his nobles that a kingdom should be ruled with justice and mercy.

Worn out by his labours and illness, Alfred died when he was only about fifty, but he left behind a free country and the ideal of the perfect king, brave, diligent and just.

'I have striven,' he said, 'to live worthily and to leave to the men who come after me, the memory of good works.'

In his lifetime, the people called him 'England's shepherd' and 'The Truth Teller'; they said 'in him the poor could look for help'. Afterwards, the English gave him a title which they have given to no other monarch in their history – Alfred the Great.

MORE ABOUT ALFRED

Alfred was born at Wantage in Berkshire in 849 and he died in 899 or 900. It was his grandfather, King Egbert (802–839), who made Wessex supreme over the other five or six kingdoms into which England had been divided for more than two centuries.

Towards the end of Egbert's reign, the Danes began to attack the coasts of England, at first as plunderers and afterwards as settlers.

Egbert's son, Ethelwulf, defeated the Danes and went on a pilgrimage to Rome, but his four sons, each of whom in turn became king of Wessex, had to defend the kingdom against the heathen invaders who had overrun the north and the east.

From 871, when he became king, to the Peace of Wedmore in 878, Alfred was engaged in a desperate struggle against Guthrum and other Danish leaders but, after his victory, Wessex consisted of about half of England, separated from the Danelaw by a line running from London to Chester. This was the kingdom which he ruled so well and which he again had to defend during his last years.

Fortunately, Alfred founded a line of splendid kings. His son, Edward the Elder, conquered the Danes and became ruler of the whole country; his grandson, Athelstan (925–940), added southern Scotland to his dominions and two more capable grandsons were followed by Edgar (954–975) whose peaceful reign and good government recalled the days of Alfred, his great-grandfather.

HAROLD, THE LAST OF THE ENGLISH

COUNT GUY of Ponthieu was supping with his knights in the rush-strewn hall of his castle when, above the gale outside, the clatter of men and arms was heard from the courtyard.

The knights grasped their weapons, but a serving-man hurried to the high table and spoke to the Count. Then the oak doors were flung open to admit a crowd of villagers and fishermen, armed with cudgels and flaring torches.

'A wreck, Sir Count!' cried their leader. 'An English ship fast on the rocks below Saint Catherine's Point. We took the crew as they came ashore through the surf.'

Count Guy glowered at the exhausted, dripping strangers who were thrust forward, some with their arms bound by ropes.

'Who are you?' he asked. 'Know you that what the sea casts up upon this coast is mine by right.'

One of the strangers, whose torn silken shirt and fair hair matted with blood did not disguise his magnificent presence, answered curtly in French,

'I am Harold Godwinson, Earl of Wessex, counsellor and kinsman to Edward, King of the English. Is this a

Christian welcome to men who have suffered shipwreck? In the name of Saint Christopher, I ask for food and shelter and a safe return to England.'

The Count's eyes narrowed as he thought of the ransom for such a prisoner.

'Bold words, stranger or spy,' he replied. 'A dog barks loud when he cannot bite. But even an English dog may be worth a price to his master. We will find out if you speak truth. Till then, you stay here at my pleasure.'

Earl Harold and his men were forced to stifle their anger while they endured several days of inhospitable treatment from the French count, but although they cursed the storm that had wrecked their ship on an unfriendly coast, not a man blamed the Earl for his whim to sail in the Channel on an autumn day. Like every man in Wessex, they loved Harold and asked only to serve him.

News of the wreck soon leaked out and, within days, a crop-headed knight rode to the castle with an order:

> *'William, duke of Normandy, bids Guy, his vassal, to send the Earl of Wessex to his Court with an escort and due honour. The Earl and his men are to be clothed and furnished with all things necessary.'*

The Count blustered about a ransom, but when the Norman knight grimly reminded him of the fate that would befall a vassal who bandied words with Duke William, he freed the prisoners with an ill grace and produced food and wine, the vestments and horses that his overlord demanded.

With a splendid company, Duke William rode to meet the English Earl, embraced him and led him to the high seat in his castle, while he smiled with a warmth that astonished the Norman knights. They knew the Duke for a hard man, grim and ruthless from his earliest years, but now he laughed.

It was strange to see William's pleasure in his handsome guest. Gifts were showered upon the Englishmen; tournaments, games and hunting-parties were held in their honour; feasts and dancing took place at night. The two nobles were well-matched; with horse and hawk, in wrestling and sword-play, men deemed them equal. Both were mighty warriors, one dark, the other fair; one hard and skilful yet determined to deal gallantly with his guest; the other so generous in his wondrous strength that even the Normans gave him praise.

The winter passed and there was no talk of going home. The festivities and tournaments were enlivened by a real battle against some of the Duke's rebellious subjects when Harold fought manfully beside his host. There seemed to be nothing but trust and affection between the two.

One day, in Spring, Harold's brother, Wulfnoth, found the Earl alone.

'Brother,' he began, 'the men would go home to England. Must we dally here so long?'

'Why, Wulfnoth,' laughed Harold. 'Are you tired of living like a prince?'

'My brother, we long for Wessex and, to speak truth, we fear this black-browed Duke with whom you pass the days. All men know that he covets England's throne and gives out that it was promised him by King Edward. Why do you stay?'

'For my own reasons, lad.'

'What reasons can there be? Edward has no son and – God forgive me – he is more monk than king. The Atheling, last of Alfred's line, is but a child. You will be King when Edward dies.'

'Hush, boy. The Witan and the word of God choose England's king.'

'Harold,' insisted Wulfnoth, 'for the love we bear you, take us home. Edward is old, the Earls and our brother Tostig make trouble while you are away. The people long for you, let us go.'

Harold absently pulled at the ears of a hunting-dog. There was a long silence and then he said, 'Come close, lad. I will tell you a secret that brought a curse upon our House. Years ago, our father, Earl Godwin, was accused of betraying King Edward's brother to the Danes. It was never proved but before he died, he told me it was true. He committed that crime for the sake of the realm, to keep the peace. It weighed heavy on our father's soul and he bade me make amends. I, too, must serve England, not by treachery but by winning the friendship of this Norman Duke. I would not have my country torn by war, so I have won William as my brother. Soon we shall part as brothers – he to remain in his own land and I to serve England as God would have me serve.'

Earl Harold asked the Duke for a ship to carry him home, but William avoided an answer. Presently, the Duke spoke of King Edward's promise of the crown; he insisted that Harold must swear to support his claim in return for half the kingdom and his daughter Agatha to wife. Until the promise was given, the guests could not go home.

Harold was trapped. Word came that King Edward was ill and the Earls were quarrelling; he must go home but he dare not swear. Old Garth, his father's steward, spoke at last,

'A forced oath, my Lord, is not binding in the sight of God. Swear, and our English priests will absolve you from the oath.'

So, before the nobles and bishops of Normandy,

Harold laid his hand upon a table covered with a cloth of gold and swore to be Duke William's man and to serve him faithfully in all things. When this was done, two priests stepped forward and removed the cloth. Beneath was not a table but a chest containing the bones of a saint. Harold and his men were horror-struck, for an oath sworn upon holy bones was no ordinary oath – forced or not, it was now a promise that filled them all with dread.

The Englishmen sailed home with heavy hearts and the story of the forced oath spread across the land. There were many who shook their heads to think that Harold had sworn away the kingdom and some remembered the curse upon his House. Yet there was no one else to rule England, for King Edward wept and babbled in his weakness; the Earls were at each other's throats and Tostig Godwinson had to be exiled for his misdeeds in the North. Harold governed the kingdom well, restoring order and justice, so that men spoke of him as a second Alfred.

Towards the end of 1065, King Edward was too ill to attend the hallowing of the Abbey at Westminster which he had spent half his life in building. In January, he died and at the end, he murmured,

'To Harold, my brother-in-law, I commit the kingdom.'

At once, the Great Council chose Harold to be King, overruling the claim of Edgar Atheling because he was a child, and giving no heed to the Norman Duke. But when the news reached Normandy, the Duke burst out in rage,

'Harold has wronged me,' he cried. 'The kingdom was mine, granted and promised as he himself has sworn. By God and the holy bones, I will take my right by war.'

All through the Spring of 1066, Duke William made ready to invade, gathering stores and arms, empressing shipwrights, enrolling knights and men-at-arms to serve him for what they might win across the narrow sea. Nor did William forget the power of the Church. He had friends in Rome, and the Pope was persuaded to bless the expedition and to send a banner. The Norman brigands felt themselves to be the knights of God.

So far, however, King Harold had little to fear. Though he had no priests to speak for him in Rome, he had the hearts of the people of England and the strong arms of the men of Wessex. His kingdom was immensely bigger and richer than Normandy. Its people had repelled many an invasion in the past and he himself, Harold the Fearless, was as great a warrior as the Duke and far superior on the sea. All that summer, Harold kept troops and ships ready to meet the invader, while he pacified the North and saw to all things with dignity and strength. Rumours came in that his brother Tostig was in Norway where Harold Hardrada, the mighty sea-robber, was fitting out his longships. What if two attacks fell upon the kingdom at the same time?

'Never fear,' Harold told his thanes. 'The same wind cannot bring both foes. If they come, we shall drub them one at a time.'

In September, the wind blew from the north; it brought the fleet of Harold Hardrada and Tostig into the Humber, where the Northmen came ashore, defeated the Earls and ravaged the countryside like wolves. King Harold marched up from the south, and, seven miles from York, at Stamford Bridge, he attacked the Norwegian host and destroyed it utterly. Among the slain were Tostig and Harold Hardrada, victor of fifty battles; but half the Huscarls and many of the best fighting men of England died as well.

While the priests sang a Victory Thanksgiving in York Minster, the wind changed in Duke William's favour. On 28th September, 1066, only three days after the battle at Stamford Bridge, the Norman fleet beached at Pevensey without so much as a fishing-boat to oppose them.

Hardly able to believe his luck, the Duke landed his horses and stores with ridiculous ease and soon the Normans were plundering Kent and Sussex to their hearts' content. Messengers fled north to Harold who lay at York, tending the wounded and resting his exhausted men.

In fury, Harold gathered all who were fit to march, and he made South at tremendous speed, outdistancing his foot-soldiers and the Northern Earls who, saying they had done enough, came only at a laggard's pace.

Once he was across the Thames, Harold had no thought but to meet his enemy and hurl him into the sea. His brothers urged caution; the King should burn the land to deny food to the invaders. Then, as soon as his footsore troops were rested, and reinforcements had come in from the West and the North, he could attack with overwhelming strength. But Harold refused to listen.

'God's Splendour!' he roared. 'Shall I burn my people's land when I promised them peace? I have whipped a pack of wolves and now will thrash these Norman dogs.'

He led his army into Sussex and set his Standard on Senlac Hill, inviting the Normans to attack. As usual, the English dismounted and ranged themselves for battle on foot. It was a strong position and Harold had his men in close order behind their shield-wall, telling them to stand firm and let the Normans exhaust themselves in uphill charges.

The royal troops, the giant Huscarls, held the middle, guarding the Standards and the King; on either flank, were the thanes and the trained men of the shires, with a sprinkling of ill-armed levies hastily raised to fill the places of men who had died in the North. But many, far too many, of England's warriors had not arrived.

The Duke attacked with archers and foot-soldiers, then with a charge by his mailed knights. The English stood firm, letting fly with javelins, stones and hand-axes, meeting the charge with level spears, while axes swung and crashed, and bowmen picked off the horses and the wounded. A second attack broke against the shield-wall, a third foundered among the piles of dead and dying. By afternoon, the Normans were almost spent.

One last charge surged up the hill and reached the shields, when a cry went up,

'The Duke is slain! Fly! Every man to the ships!'

A roar burst from the English and the levies leapt from their ranks and tore after the retreating foe but, in the valley, William checked the flight and sent horsemen from the flanks to ride down the men of the shires.

On the hill, the staunch axe-men still stood beside their King. Then the Duke ordered his bowmen to fire upwards so that their arrows fell in a deadly rain. Harold was struck above the right eye, and the whole line groaned when he fell.

Darkness was coming on when the Norman knights breached the English wall, cutting down those who had not fled. At last, only a knot of Huscarls was left, wielding their axes with matchless courage round the Standard of Wessex and their dying King. They fought on to the last man.

It was night when the Duke's servants pitched his tent

The Battle of Hastings

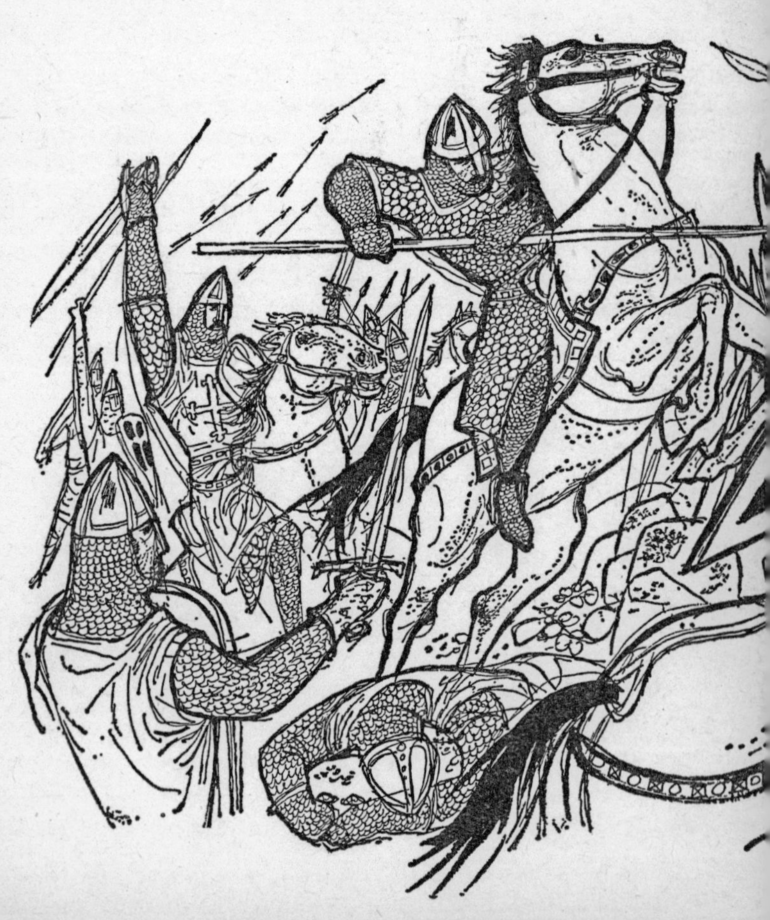

where the battle had been fiercest, and the Conqueror, speechless with fatigue, sat down among the slain. Outside, somewhere in the darkness, lay the bodies of Harold, his brothers and the noblest men of England. In a single day, the kingdom had been lost and won.

MORE ABOUT HAROLD

Harold was the son of Earl Godwin, an Englishman who rose to a position of power under Canute, the Danish King of England. Harold's mother was a relative of Canute himself.

When Canute died in 1035, there was a period of confusion until 1042 when Edward (afterwards called the Confessor) came over from Normandy where he had been brought up in exile. Although Edward was descended from Alfred the Great and although he married Godwin's daughter, his Norman friends gained power so that Godwin had to flee to Flanders with two of his sons. Harold took refuge in Ireland. It was at this time, that William of Normandy visited England and received the so-called promise of the English crown.

Soon afterwards, Earl Godwin and his sons returned to favour and, during the latter part of the Confessor's reign, Harold and his younger brothers practically ruled the kingdom.

Harold had already distinguished himself as a warrior and statesman when, in 1064, he was so unluckily wrecked on the French coast and fell into William's power.

However, chosen by the Witan and named by Edward on his deathbed in January 1066, Harold was the rightful King of England. He possessed the character to have made a splendid ruler but he was dogged by ill-luck.

Contrary winds prevented William from sailing in the summer when he would have stood little chance against the English fleet and army that awaited him. Tostig's treachery not only drew Harold north and cost him some of his best troops, but it allowed William to land unopposed. Even so, Harold should not have been defeated if he had waited to build up his forces instead of trusting everything to a single battle.

MONTEZUMA, KING OF THE AZTECS

'I SPEAK truth, your Honour, when I say that with my own eyes I saw a land far richer than this island of Cuba. The people dwell in houses of stone and eat from platters of gold. But, beyond the mountains, they say there is a treasure-city in a land called Mexico, ruled by the Great King Montezuma.'

The speaker paused and Senor Valazquez, Governor of Cuba, answered him, 'You bring great news, Don Pedro,' and his eyes shone. 'In the name of the Holy Virgin and of His Imperial Majesty, we shall send an expedition to discover the riches of this land.'

Valazquez looked round at the Spanish gentlemen who were gathered in the Governor's House; his eye fell upon Hernan Cortes, one of the settlers in Cuba who, it was well-known, preferred adventure to the easy life of a slave-run estate. Cortes was the man to lead a search for gold.

The year was 1518. More than twenty-five years had passed since Columbus reached the New World but, so far, Spain had gained only a few islands. Little gold had been discovered and the mainland of America had only been touched here and there by adventurers like Pedro. His news sent hopes soaring again.

By February 1519, Cortes had assembled eleven small ships manned by 100 sailors, with 553 adventurers, mostly gentlemen who contributed money and arms to the expedition. The ships were loaded with stores, armour, gunpowder, crossbows, 14 cannon, some mastiff dogs and 16 horses. The Governor and all the aristocracy of Cuba came to see the expedition set sail, but during the high-sounding speeches, it was noticed that Cortes seemed to be occupied with his own thoughts.

Hernan Cortes was 34 years old; tall, lean and broad-shouldered, he wore a black beard that partly hid the scar of an old knife wound and, though his manner was courteous, his grey eyes were hard. He had come out to the West Indies from Spain as a lad of 19, but, although he had done well enough, this was his first real chance to win the fame and riches he longed for with all his soul.

The little fleet sighted the mainland of Central America and sailed along the coast until a suitable place was found for a landing.

A strong army of Maya Indians attacked the Spaniards with ferocious courage, but Cortes made such brilliant use of his cannons and horses, neither of which the Mayas had ever seen before, that the natives surrendered.

Peace gifts were brought, including twenty slave-girls, among whom was an intelligent maiden called Marina. Daughter of an Aztec or Mexican chief, she had been stolen as a child and sold into slavery, but now she was to become the devoted companion of Cortes. Marina learned Spanish, acted as an interpreter and adviser and behaved with complete coolness amid the worst dangers because she believed that the gods had chosen her to bring ruin upon her own people.

As the expedition continued along the coast, Cortes asked Marina to tell him about the Aztecs.

'My people are the most powerful race in Mexico,' she said. 'All the surrounding tribes pay taxes to Montezuma, the Great King.'

'What kind of taxes?'

'Cotton cloth, maize, chocolate and honey; incense, tobacco, feathers of every colour, jewels, gold and jade.'

'Are your people brave warriors?'

'O, Captain-General, they never cease from war. War is necessary to obtain prisoners.'

'But why do they need prisoners? For slaves?'

'For slaves, yes. But chiefly for the gods. Unless the gods are fed with human hearts, plucked warm from the bodies of men, disaster would come upon the kingdom.'

The ships anchored off the coast of Mexico and at once two large canoes appeared with messengers who were friendly and strangely respectful. Presently, they hurried away inland to report to King Montezuma, while the Spaniards built a camp on the shore.

Within a week, the envoys returned, accompanied by a string of porters loaded with gifts. There were jewels and masks of solid gold, precious ornaments shaped like jaguars and monkeys, bracelets, necklaces, and gold collars, capes made of brilliant feathers and two gigantic circles, one of silver, one of gold, covered with carvings and sacred signs. But the envoys said that Montezuma did not wish to see the strangers. They must go away and not attempt to visit his capital.

Cortes pondered. For some reason, the Aztecs feared him and were bribing him to go away, but the gifts

Great riches were offered to Cortes

proved that this land was richer than anyone had dared to hope. He would certainly go forward, trusting to luck and his own daring.

Montezuma's envoys vanished, but messengers arrived from a neighbouring tribe which had recently been conquered by the Aztecs. These people and their king, known as Fat Lord, were anxious to make friends with the strangers, having already heard about their magic weapons.

Cortes told Fat Lord to arrest Montezuma's tax-gatherers and to send no more people for human sacrifice. Moreover, he ordered his new allies to stop their own horrible sacrifices and he boldly threw down the image of the Maize God from the top of a lofty pyramid-temple. The terrified people obeyed him in everything, even setting up a Cross and an image of the Virgin Mary.

Meanwhile, in his distant capital, the very thought of the strangers on the coast filled Montezuma with dread. His life, his kingdom and all his riches existed solely to please the gods, especially Humming Bird, the terrible god of war. Unless they were regularly fed with human hearts, the gods would die. Then the Sun would go out, the Rains would cease, the Wind would sweep everything away. But long, long ago, there had been a god named Quetzalcoatl (the Feathered Serpent) who had been driven out by the others; in the year of One Reed, Quetzalcoatl would return to claim his kingdom. He would come from the east on a curious raft; his skin would be white, his beard black; he would not eat human hearts but his coming would bring ruin and great sorrow.

In dread, therefore, Montezuma listened to the bearers of bad news who bowed themselves to the ground and were taken away to be killed. 1519 *was* the year of One Reed and the strangers had landed on the exact day worked out by the wizards of the calendar, The leader was white-skinned, black-bearded; his followers carried rods of lightning whose iron barrels spoke thunder.

Exactly as the sacred books foretold, there had been comets, floods and earthquakes. As expected, the strangers wore hats of iron and were accompanied by four-legged creatures and by smaller animals, as fierce as jaguars, with rolling eyes and lolling tongues.

It was terrifyingly clear that Quetzalcoatl had come.

Montezuma dared not attack a god. It seemed as if Mexico was doomed whatever action he took. Nevertheless, he sent gifts, hoping that the strangers would depart, and he also sent wizards, sorcerers and man-witches, but their magic had no effect whatever on the grey-eyed leader. So Montezuma, wise and gentle in all other ways, tried sacrifice of the most horrible kind, using his own hands to sprinkle blood on the altars of the gods, but there was no answer.

He must await the pleasure of Quetzalcoatl.

Knowing nothing of these dark mysteries, Cortes prepared to advance on the capital. He had the ships run ashore and totally destroyed to convince his men that there was no retreat. Ahead lay riches or death.

Leaving a small garrison at a fort on the coast which he named Vera Cruz, Cortes set off on the 250-mile journey, with 400 men, 15 horses and the cannons that were carried by porters provided by Fat Lord.

The march took the conquerers through fertile country dotted with neat maize fields, across mountain passes and desert stretches. They were baked by the sun and frozen by icy winds in the mountains. They were often hungry and always thirsty, but their remorseless leader marched on.

Presently, they entered the territory of the fierce Tlaxcalans, the only people in the region whom Montezuma had not conquered. Since they hated the Aztecs, they attacked the strangers who were travelling to Mexico City, but as warriors, they were superstitious and apt to lose heart.

All Mexican warfare aimed at taking prisoners alive so that they could be sacrificed later, but the Spaniards refused to be captured and fought like demons with weapons far superior to slings and wooden swords edged with sharp flakes of stone. Moreover, the Mexicans were badly led, whereas Cortes was a soldier of genius, cool, fearless and absolutely certain of victory.

Having beaten off an ambush, Cortes boldly attacked the Tlaxcalan main army with such ferocity that all the rumours about him being a god seemed to be true. Since it was useless to fight against gods, the Tlaxcalans gave up the struggle and offered him their help against Montezuma.

So, reinforced by 6,000 allies, the Spaniards marched on to Cholula, a most beautiful city, sacred to Quetzalcoatl himself, whose vast pyramid-temple dominated the countryside. Against the advice of Marina and the Tlaxcalans, Cortes entered the city with only his 400 conquerors, leaving his allies camped outside the walls, but although he was received with friendliness, there were rumours and preparations that made him uneasy. Marina whispered that he had walked into a trap, and, at once, he sent a runner to the camp with a message,

'When I give the signal, attack the city! Break in and kill!'

This was just what the Tlaxcalans wanted and they

tore through the streets looting and killing until 6,000 Cholulans perished and the city was a smoking ruin.

Since all Aztec gods were cruel, this savage deed convinced everyone that Quetzalcoatl had come to take his revenge. At all costs, his anger must be soothed and Montezuma sent slaves loaded with gifts and messages,

'The Great Montezuma sends his loving greetings. He is sorry that the stupid Cholulans offended you, but he offers you his capital. Come, Great One, and rest quietly.'

On to Mexico!

The conquerors crossed a lofty pass between smoking volcanoes and there, below them, lay the fabulous city, its white buildings and gigantic temples reflected in the waters of a lake. Three long roads or causeways connected Mexico City to the mainland, but, for defence, these were broken by several drawbridges and a fleet of war-canoes patrolled the lake.

The Spaniards clattered across the widest causeway, the horsemen riding ahead. Then came the chained mastiffs, the lean, grim swordsmen, the crossbowmen and the musketeers, all warily fingering their weapons as they passed between rows of citizens who murmured in awe at the sight of such strange beings.

At the city walls, Montezuma himself came forward. Beneath a wondrous canopy, his golden throne was carried by eight lords in magnificent robes and he himself was wearing a jewelled crown topped by green plumes, a feather cloak and vestments that glittered with precious stones; even the soles of his sandals were made of pure gold.

The two men gazed at each other; both were handsome, both held themselves like men born to command.

But whereas Montezuma's eyes were troubled by the deep fears of his terrible religion, Cortes showed only the watchful calm of a man who had dared everything to reach his goal.

'Welcome to my capital, Great One,' said Montezuma. 'My father's palace is your resting-place. Come, all things are yours.'

Never, in all their travels, had the Spaniards seen such a city. It was beautiful beyond their dreams; canals criss-crossed the broad avenues and smooth streets, fountains played in noble courtyards where banks of flowers blazed in the warm sunshine; the luxury of the houses astounded men who had seen the cities of Italy and France.

The palace, near to Montezuma's and to the temple of the Humming Bird, was enormous; its one hundred bedrooms each had running water and a stone bath; the ceilings were encrusted with carvings, and the floors gleamed like mirrors. In the throne-room, the walls were decorated with bands of silver and gold inset with precious stones. Cortes noticed that the courtyards were big enough to hold an army or perhaps to trap an army. He was now in a fortress-palace of a lake-city, with a handful of soldiers. What should he do next? What was Montezuma planning?

For several days, the Spaniards toured the city, observing its defences and its vast colourful markets. The two leaders paid each other visits, exchanging courteous conversation, while each tried to read the other's mind. Montezuma was puzzled by talk of an Emperor across the sea and by the Christian religion. Cortes admired the city, but made it clear that he was horrified by the temples with their racks of skulls and hideous images reeking of blood, though the King was quick to see that gold put him into a good humour.

Suddenly, Cortes decided to capture Montezuma, for he could think of no other way out of his difficulties. Boldly he went to the Great King and accused him of ordering an attack on the Spaniards at Vera Cruz. Montezuma gently denied the accusation and immediately sent runners to the coast to make sure that all was well, but Cortes insisted that he must come and live in the Spaniards' palace.

'But my lords would never consent,' pleaded Montezuma. 'What would my people say?'

'You must tell them that it is your own wish. Say the gods have commanded it.'

Montezuma submitted. The god had spoken, he must obey. Perhaps if he pleased him, he might still go away and the people would be saved.

With Montezuma in his power, Cortes began to rule. He put down a rising, had two sloops built and launched on the lake, sent men to inspect the country, especially the gold-mines, and he had a statue of the Virgin placed in one of the temples. Oddly enough, the more the Spaniards saw of Montezuma, the more they loved the sad, noble king. He was so gentle and his generosity was princely compared with Cortes', who was stinginess itself when it came to sharing treasure.

News from the coast forced Cortes to leave the city with most of his force in order to deal with a rival expedition from Cuba, which he quickly overcame with his usual boldness and cunning. But when he returned, he found that Pedro, his deputy-commander, was in a tight corner, for the townsfolk had broken into rebellion once the god-man had departed. Because of Montezuma's influence, Cortes and his soldiers regained the fortress without difficulty, but the city was seething with rumours that a new King had been elected.

Presently, the Aztecs attacked the palace, firing

arrows and spears from the house-tops, hurling stones from slings and primitive machines, leaping from the walls with frenzied courage. There was fierce hand-to-hand fighting in which muskets and cannons were useless, but Cortes retook the walls and made several sorties into the streets.

The Mexicans ignored their losses and kept up the attack until, after five days, Cortes could see that his force would soon be worn down. There was only one thing to do; he would tell Montezuma to stop the fighting so that the white men could depart peacefully.

'It will be of no use,' said Montezuma sadly. 'My people have chosen another King. They will not let you escape.'

He still believed that Cortes was a god, but he knew now that the other gods had won back their power. He himself was fated to obey Quetzalcoatl. So he put on his gorgeous robes and his plumed crown and went up to the walls. At once, the Mexicans ceased to attack when they saw his beloved figure and some fell upon their knees as he began to speak.

Suddenly, a volley of stones was fired by the slingers. Montezuma fell and was carried down to his apartment, where he was found to have a severe head wound but, worse, he clearly had no wish to live.

Next day, Montezuma died, and even as they fought, the hard-bitten Spaniards wept for him.

The end of Montezuma was not quite the end of the story. By superhuman efforts, the Spaniards fought their way out of the capital, losing half their men in a desperate night battle along a causeway. Eventually a handful of survivors reached the land of the Tlaxcalans where they were given shelter.

But Cortes was not beaten. He obtained troops and supplies from the Spanish islands, raised a huge army from the tribes and built a fleet of ships to cross the lake. In the following year, after a tremendous struggle, the beautiful city was captured and utterly destroyed, and Cortes claimed Mexico for the Emperor Charles V of Spain.

MORE ABOUT MONTEZUMA

Montezuma II (1466–1520) succeeded his uncle as king of Mexico, but although he was a powerful ruler, he seems to have earned the hatred of the neighbouring tribes. This explains why Cortes received so much help from the Tlaxcalans.

The Aztecs were originally a tribe of hunters from the north and they had settled in Mexico about 200 years before the arrival of Cortes. Quickly conquering the surrounding peoples, they had built the wonderful lake-city which they called Tenochtitlan. Theirs was a strange civilization, for although they were skilful architects and craftsmen who understood trade and mathematics, they had no wheel nor any form of transport except boats; metals were hardly used and iron was quite unknown.

Hernando Cortes (1485–1547) was the son of a poor nobleman; at 19, he threw up his law-studies and went to seek his fortune in the West Indies. After distinguishing himself during the conquest of Cuba, he had to wait 10 years for the chance to win fame and gold. After Mexico had fallen, he was granted a title and estates but he always felt that his great achievements were not fully recognized. He visited Spain and was honoured by Charles V, took part in various voyages and adventures in which he lost much of his wealth and died, sad and neglected, in his own country. Our knowledge of Montezuma and Cortes comes from one of the survivors of the little band of conquerors, who, as an old man, wrote down all that he remembered about the amazing adventure.

WILLIAM THE SILENT

THE name of Holland's national hero suggests a brooding, iron-jawed leader, but William the Silent was really a gay and charming prince who was not even a Dutchman. His story is as curious as his nickname.

William was born in Germany at the castle of Dillenburg whose old-fashioned turrets overtopped the roofs of a pleasant village near to the River Rhine. His father, the Count of Nassau, had married a beautiful widow named Juliana, and William, born in 1533, the same year as Elizabeth Tudor, was the eldest son of a large family.

The castle was a lively home, full of children, governesses, tutors, grooms and riding-masters, for Juliana not only presided over her family with loving devotion, but she formed a school at the castle, inviting children from noble families in the district to ride in for lessons. The Count was not rich, but he busied himself on his estates, taking more interest in farming and in the welfare of his people than in the quarrels of the German princelings.

The Dillenburg children were brought up to plain fare and to the enjoyment of family games and country festivities. William and his brothers, especially John and Louis who were nearest to him in age, learned to ride and hunt with their neighbours but, above all, their mother taught them to behave with kindness and dignity, to love justice and to respect the opinions of others.

At this time, the religious teaching of Luther and Calvin was sweeping across Germany into France, the Netherlands and England, much to the alarm of Roman Catholic rulers who saw in the Protestant religion a threat to their own power. The Emperor Charles V began to punish heretics with death, but at Dillenburg, although the Count and his wife became Protestants, life went along quietly enough until William reached the age of eleven.

An astonishing piece of news reached the castle. A rich cousin had been killed in France and all his wealth was left to William. By a fluke, the boy became one of the richest nobles in Europe, far higher in rank than his own father. His new-found fortune included hundreds of estates, great stretches of land in France, Italy and the Netherlands, with the title Prince of Orange from the name of a small principality in the south of France which William never visited in his whole life.

The young prince could no longer stay at Dillenburg. Custom demanded that he should be brought up at the Emperor's Court at Brussels, so William said good-bye to his brothers and sisters and to his mother who prayed, amid her tears, that he would not forget the lessons she had taught him. The boy rode with his father to the Netherlands and there was handed into the care of the tutors, priests and gentlemen-in-waiting who had been specially chosen by the Emperor himself.

The magnificence of the Court was a startling change from Dillenburg, but if William was homesick, he did not show it. The merry, handsome boy accepted his new life with such eager charm that he soon became a favourite with everyone. Charles V so delighted in his company that he would keep him by his side, even when the greatest courtiers had to withdraw from the royal presence. When the Emperor was away, his sister, the Regent of the Netherlands, looked after the boy with tender affection and took him with her to the cities and villages of the Low Countries.

At this time, the Netherlands consisted of modern Belgium and Holland, seventeen provinces that made up the richest country in Europe. There were more than two hundred towns, most of them walled and semi-independent, and the people, under their proud nobles, were boisterous and hard-working. Their wealth came from the skill of the weavers and tapestry-makers, from trade with Germany and the Baltic, from farming and fishing, from moneylending and banking.

These lively people were ruled by the Emperor, and the wealth of their cities was absolutely essential to him, for, despite his possessions in Austria, Italy and Spain, despite the gold from the New World, he was always short of money for his wars.

William, Prince of Orange, grew up into a gay leader of fashion. He built himself several palaces where the dazzling extravagance of his parties became famous. The Emperor chose an heiress to be his bride, made him governor, or Stadtholder, of three provinces and Commander-in-Chief of an army.

At the age of 20, William was campaigning in the war against France, taking part in sieges and night-attacks, enduring the life of camp and fortress. He also learned about the sufferings of common soldiers and did all he could to ease their hardships. But he hated the looting of captured towns and he was constantly asking the Emperor to send pay for the soldiers who otherwise had to steal. Most of all, he was sickened by the horrors of public executions and the burning alive of humble citizens who had, he knew, committed no crime except that of worshipping as Protestants.

In William, the fashionable world saw a gifted prince, blessed by fortune and good looks, a man whose courtesy was as remarkable as his kindness to servants and even to criminals. He lived like a prince, but underneath all his extravagance and easy charm, there was still the open-hearted boy of Dillenburg whose mother had taught him to love justice.

Charles V suddenly decided to give up all his titles to retire to a monastery. Leaning on the arm of his beloved William, the weary Emperor handed over his power to his son, Philip II of Spain, who came to Brussels for the ceremony. Philip was thin and ugly; he seldom spoke or looked anyone in the face and he was a fanatic. The one object of his life was to crush the Protestant religion and to stamp out its beliefs by torture and the sword.

Philip immediately sensed that his father's favourite was at heart an opponent, but for the moment he showed favour to William. When the war with France was ended, he sent him to Paris to arrange the terms of the peace treaty and here, as usual, William enjoyed the luxury of a brilliant Court.

One day, he was out hunting with the royal party and by chance found himself alone in the woods with King Henry II of France. The king began to speak of a secret that lay on his mind. In horrified amazement, William heard him describe Philip's plan for the two monarchs to use Spanish soldiers to massacre the Protestants in their countries, beginning with the stubborn Netherlanders. But though deeply shocked, William gave no sign, beyond a murmur of polite interest, so Henry never suspected that under that courteous manner, William was burning with indignation.

Later, he said he felt overcome 'with pity and compassion for all these good people doomed to destruction'. This moment was the turning-point of his life. Yet, for the time being, he said nothing – as his enemies always declared, no-one knew his thoughts; he was sly, he was William 'the Silent'.

Soon afterwards, Philip decided to go back to Spain, but first he must have a huge sum of money from the Netherlanders whose Parliament, called the Estates, granted it, providing he would take his soldiers with him. Furious, he had to agree but, as he was about to sail, he turned to Orange who was bidding him a courteous farewell, and bitterly complained about the impudent Netherlanders. 'It was the decision of the Estates, my Lord,' replied Orange gently.

Philip lost all control and snatched the nobleman's sleeve while he jabbed him with an accusing finger, 'Not the Estates,' he hissed. 'But you, you, you!'

In the absence of the king, the Netherlands were governed by his sister, the Regent, and a Council of State, but the real ruler was Cardinal Granvelle. This priest was so greedy and cunning that the Dutch nobles, led by Count Egmont, began to mock his extravagance, calling themselves 'the Beggars' in derision.

At last, Philip was obliged to recall Granvelle but he made up his mind to crush these uppish Netherlanders. Men were forbidden to be Protestants or even to discuss the Scriptures and anyone suspected of heresy was tortured and put to death.

So far, the Prince of Orange had kept quiet. The

Spaniards distrusted him, because he was so widely loved by the people, but he had never sided openly with the Beggars and he was still a Roman Catholic, though he believed that men should worship as they chose. The situation grew worse and William resigned his governorships and retired to Dillenburg.

It was just as well. The Duke of Alva arrived with an army of Spanish soldiers; Egmont was executed, William's estates were seized and his eldest son was kidnapped and taken away to Spain. The Netherlands suffered a ghastly wave of terror as Alva rooted out the Protestants, with cruel relish: 'I have tamed men of iron,' he boasted, 'shall I not now be able to tame men of butter?'

More than 18,000 died for their religion and thousands more fled to Germany and England.

At Dillenburg, where Juliana still exercised her gentle rule, the family rejoiced to have William home after so many years. He could do little at first, except appeal for help to Elizabeth Tudor and the German princes, but he knew that cruelty was not stamping out the Protestant faith in the Netherlands. It burned all the more fiercely, and he himself turned to that religion.

After four years of exile, he raised an army of refugees and hired soldiers, selling his jewels and plate to help find the money. Then he set off with his brothers Louis, Adolphus and Henry, to make war against the Spanish tyrant.

But the Protestant force was small and many of the mercenaries were faint-hearted. The prince lost battle after battle; his brother Adolphus was killed and Alva laid waste the countryside.

Presently William was forced to wander about, too weak to make a major attack, but always hoping to hear news of help from the French Protestants (the

Huguenots) who had powerful leaders and great hopes. But on St. Bartholomew's Eve 1572, a terrible massacre in Paris destroyed the Huguenot cause, and William, with only 70 men left, was forced to retreat into the northern provinces of Zealand and Holland, where, amid canals and islands, it was difficult for the Spaniards to follow. Alva was triumphant everywhere and towns like Haarlem that defied him were put to the sword.

William did not despair even when his position was hopeless. Once, he was asked if there was any chance of an alliance with a foreign power. 'I have entered into a close alliance with God,' he replied. 'And I am firmly convinced that all who put their trust in Him shall be saved by His almighty hand.'

He was saved, not by an army, but by a fleet composed of fishing-boats manned by the seafaring folk of the northern provinces. Calling themselves the Sea-Beggars, they began to work along the coast, attacking Spanish ships and destroying Philip's reinforcements. By a bold stroke, they captured the port of Brill which gave them a valuable base from which to carry out their raids, and they often slipped into Dover to sell the booty, for Elizabeth turned a blind eye to their exploits and was secretly sending arms and men to William.

As the tide turned and towns held out against the Spaniards, Alva lost heart and resigned his command. William advanced and captured an important fortress, while his brothers Louis and Henry were leading a small army from Germany. He waited for their arrival, but there was no news. Days passed and then came the awful tidings that both brothers had been killed in a desperate charge against the enemy.

This disaster allowed the Spaniards to besiege Leyden, a prosperous town, some six miles from the sea and vital to the defence of the north. The town was completely surrounded and though the townsfolk held out behind their battered walls, their valiant Burgomaster knew they could barely last a month. William had no soldiers left and he could only send in messages by carrier pigeon until he fell so ill from fever that men despaired of his life.

Leyden held on, for a month, for two months and the people began to die of hunger. At last, Orange asked the Estates to cut the dykes and let the sea flow across their precious fields, so that the Sea-Beggars could sail in to the rescue. 'Better a drowned land than a lost land,' they cried, and the dykes were cut.

The sea crept in and the dismayed Spaniards fled from the rising waters as the ships manoeuvred between the trees and farm roofs.

Now William went to live in Delft with his wife and children, no longer rich but loved by everyone, and he worked with all his soul to unite the provinces. It was a slow task, for the Dutch loved independence and the south was still Catholic. But when 8,000 Spanish troops made an attack on Antwerp so savage that it was known ever afterwards as 'the Spanish Fury', the Estates agreed to form a Union of all the provinces.

This was the greatest triumph of William's career. The Spaniards retreated and he entered Brussels after ten years' absence through streets lined with the cheering populace.

To hold the Netherlands together, a monarch was needed. William refused the crown because he wished to serve rather than to rule, but he hoped that Elizabeth of England might accept. When she refused, he persuaded the Estates to invite a French prince, the Duke of Anjou, an absurd little fellow, as ugly as a bull-frog and quite untrustworthy.

Anjou arrived, full of promises and fair speeches, but within a year, he was gone, driven out for his miserable treachery. Meanwhile, as the Spaniards recovered, the South wavered and fell away. The northern provinces formed a separate Union and William went back to live

Better a drowned land than a lost land

in Delft. In this town of canals and quiet streets, 'Father' William was often to be seen, walking along deep in thought, his handsome head now grey and his once-gorgeous clothes as shabby as those of any poor townsman.

There was much to worry about; he had not been well since a would-be assassin shot him in the face at Antwerp, but he had to work ceaselessly to persuade the cities and provinces to stay united. He persuaded; he would never force or bully. But the Spaniards, under a brilliant general, the Duke of Parma, were steadily winning back the South and drawing nearer to the United Provinces.

Still, there was much to be thankful for. The people trusted Orange and loved him, though they made him sad when they repaid cruelty with cruelty. He wanted freedom for all men and he hoped, for he was only fifty, that he had many years left in which to serve his adopted country. He did not reckon with the dark mind of a fanatic.

The Spaniards regularly employed spies and assassins, but even they would not pay money to Balthazar Gerard, a crack-witted apprentice who had vowed to kill the Prince of Orange. Somehow, Gerard reached Delft where, pretending to be the son of a murdered Protestant, he got to know a friend of the prince, was employed by him as a messenger, and, once, he actually entered William's house, only to find that he had no weapon.

Gerard hung about the courtyard, chatting to the guards and telling them that he would enlist in the Protestant forces if only he could afford a pair of stout shoes. This was reported to Orange who, with his usual generosity, sent down a sum of money to the poor messenger.

Next day, Gerard bought a pair of pistols and returned to the courtyard. After dinner, as the prince was leaving his room by an outside staircase, the assassin stepped from an archway and fired twice into his body. William staggered and gasped, 'My God, have pity on my soul; my God, have pity upon my poor people.' He was dead by the time they had carried him indoors.

Gerard was caught and put to a horrible death, smiling and praying to the end, but William the Silent was buried in the great bare church of Delft, where he still lies under the canopy of a marble tomb, with an angel sounding a trumpet above his head. He had been called 'the wisest, gentlest and bravest man who ever led a nation' and when he died, the little children cried in the streets.

MORE ABOUT WILLIAM

When William the Silent (1533–1584) went as a boy of eleven to the Court at Brussels, the Emperor Charles V was the greatest monarch in Europe. As Holy Roman Emperor, he had great possessions in Germany and power over many of the princes; he ruled Austria and the Netherlands, he was king of Spain with all its colonies and the kingdoms of Sicily and Naples. These huge territories caused him endless trouble for he was opposed by France, by the Turks and by the Protestants in Germany and the Netherlands. At last, worn out, he retired to a Spanish monastery and died there in 1558.

Although William did not live to complete his task of freeing the Dutch people from Spanish rule, his sons, Maurice and Frederick Henry, carried on his work. For a time, it seemed as if the Duke of Parma must defeat them, despite the help sent by Elizabeth from England. However, Parma had to prepare an army to invade England and, after the Armada, Philip ordered him to France.

Meanwhile, William's son, known as Maurice of Nassau, proved himself the best soldier in Europe and the Dutch fleet grew ever stronger. By 1609, Spain had to agree to a twelve years' truce and in 1648, the Netherlands (known as the Dutch United Provinces and, later, as Holland) finally won their freedom.

ELIZABETH OF ENGLAND

ON a November day in 1558, Elizabeth rode into London. The gorgeous procession, headed by the Lord Mayor and the Garter King-at-Arms, wound slowly through streets hung with tapestries and silks. The narrow way was jammed with citizens who shouted with joy for their new Queen and also with relief that her sister was dead.

Cannon boomed down the river as Elizabeth came to the Tower of London. Turning to those about her, she said,

'I am raised from being a prisoner in this place to being a Prince of this land.'

From babyhood, her life had been in danger. She had known four stepmothers, a brother surrounded by scheming nobles, a sister hated for her religion and her Spanish husband. In a world of plots and treachery, she had been imprisoned, questioned and spied upon, so that she knew more about lies than truth, more about the value of keeping silent than about love and kindness.

But the lonely, frightened child had grown into a striking woman who looked every inch a queen.

In the minds of the cheering Londoners, there was no doubt that this was Henry VIII's daughter. They could see that in the reddish tint of her curly hair, in the firm set of her mouth, in the shrewd blue eyes that looked everywhere and missed nothing. Her manner reminded them of the great Henry. Now and then, she paused majestically to let the people see her in her jewels and purple velvet; she picked out someone in the crowd to praise, another to pity. She replied wittily to a compliment and then hurled back a coarse jest to some brawny carter waving to her from a barrel-top. The crowd roared with laughter:

'God save your Grace!' they bellowed.

'God bless you all, good people!' answered the Queen.

But Elizabeth had heard cheers before. She remembered how her sister Mary had been cheered only five years ago, and now she was dead, a tragic failure.

The kingdom had sunk low in those five years and now was only 'a bone between two dogs' – France and Spain. The people were divided by religious hatred, the Treasury was empty, the warships were rotten and the French had captured Calais. But Spain was equally interested in controlling England, for Queen Mary had married Philip II of Spain, so, if French troops landed, Spanish armies would surely follow.

Thus, in 1558, it seemed certain that Elizabeth's reign would be short and bloody. She was only twenty-five and she had no powerful friends to help her; half the people were still Roman Catholics at heart, believing that the rightful queen was Mary Queen of Scots, now in France. Nevertheless, Elizabeth faced the situation bravely.

First, she found advisers who could be trusted. She kept some of the nobles who had served Mary, but she also chose men from the middle-class, solid, faithful men like William Cecil, her greatest minister, Nicholas Bacon, Thomas Gresham and Walsingham, the master of her secret service.

The nobles and courtiers who made the Court so gay and colourful, men such as Leicester, Raleigh, Sidney and Essex, were given fine-sounding appointments. Yet, although she delighted in the company of handsome young men and kept them always close to the throne, Elizabeth never told them the innermost secrets or gave them the trust that she gave to quiet Cecil.

England's new Queen had to settle the religious struggle by somehow satisfying the Protestants without driving the Roman Catholics into rebellion. She herself could not understand why men should torture and kill each other for religion – once she wrote to Philip:

'What does it matter to your Majesty if they go to the Devil in their own way?'

So, as long as people went regularly to Church of England services and did not openly worship as Roman Catholics, Elizabeth did not inquire closely into their beliefs. She wanted religious peace, and for eleven years, no-one in the realm was executed for religion or treason.

Money was the next pressing problem. Kings were expected to keep up a handsome Court and to pay for most of the country's expenses out of their own pockets, for Parliament met only from time to time to make special 'grants' for such expenses as wars. Prices were going up and the Queen's income, mostly from the rents of farms on her estates, stood still.

So, for the whole of her reign, Elizabeth had to pinch and scrape to make ends meet. She earned a name for being mean and it was even said that she kept her sailors short of powder and shot. The truth was that she was careful about money because she would not grind her people with heavy taxes and she hated waste. She sold much of her own land and died poorer than at her Coronation.

In Thomas Gresham, the Queen found a man who was a genius with money and she gave the people a new coinage in place of the clipped coins that hampered trade because no-one trusted their value. Above all, she avoided war. Kings, nobles and even common citizens loved the glory and excitement of war, but she, a woman, knew better. It was risky and expensive.

By every possible means, Elizabeth kept out of wars. She made no threats or defiant speeches to her enemies. When she had to act, she acted craftily, sending 'underhand' help to the Dutch Protestants and French Huguenots, but always unofficially, so that she could say she knew nothing when an angry king accused her of aiding his rebellious subjects. She encouraged her sea-dogs to rob and her merchant-adventurers to trade, often providing ships and some of the cost of an expedition so that she could take her share of the profits. But if her captains ran into trouble with the Spaniards or the Portuguese, that was their affair.

When it suited her, Elizabeth was all innocence about the behaviour of her subjects in the English Channel or on the Spanish Main. She would promise to find out, she would punish; but she did nothing. The Spanish ambassador fumed and wrote to his master:

'This woman is possessed of a hundred thousand devils.'

Craftiness and silence were two of Elizabeth's qualities that infuriated her friends and enemies alike. Poor Cecil was always begging her to make up her mind; so were the Scots, the Dutch, the French, King Philip and all the princes who wanted to marry her. But she would not answer. She would put off a decision until the morrow in case something better turned up. Then she would take a different course, change the subject and laugh at her grave statesmen as she turned to flirt with the courtiers who hovered about her like so many gorgeous butterflies. Few of them realized that this maddening, enchanting Queen was playing her own game.

Elizabeth played for time. By trickery and lies, with courage and love, she was steering her country out of its troubles, but time was everything.

At first, there was more danger from France than from Spain. King Philip certainly offered to marry Elizabeth and she pretended to consider the matter, though she had no intention of repeating her sister's mistake. For years, she kept on good and even affectionate terms with Philip, because neither wanted a war and both were frightened of France.

The French King had captured Calais; his son had married the beautiful young Mary Queen of Scots and his troops were looking after Scotland in her absence. It seemed only a matter of time before he would place her on the thrones of both Scotland and England.

But a storm drowned another French army that was on its way to Scotland and the Scottish Protestants, with cautious help from Elizabeth, were able to drive out the French Regent and her soldiers. Then came news that the French King had been killed in an accident, and therefore Mary was Queen of France, Queen of Scotland and, she claimed, Queen of England too.

Elizabeth's luck held. Mary was soon a widow and she had to return to Scotland where she made a disastrous marriage with Lord Darnley, her worthless cousin. Darnley was murdered and when Mary married the man who probably killed him, a worse ruffian named Bothwell, the Scots were so angry that they drove the pair out of the kingdom.

Penniless and without so much as a change of clothes,

Mary escaped to England and appealed to her cousin Elizabeth for help.

Elizabeth sent a paltry gift of clothing but no promises, for, although she disliked rebellion, she was not eager to help a rival who had claimed her own throne. So she did nothing, apart from keeping Mary a prisoner in various castles for eighteen years.

It was a dangerous policy, for, as long as Mary was alive, Catholics at home and abroad plotted to rescue her. There was a rebellion in the North and the rebels were punished with horrible severity. For once, Elizabeth showed a glimpse of her father's savage temper, but she was badly frightened – not for herself, she was never scared of assassins – but for the kingdom. If the revolt had been successful, there would have been civil war, and England would have been a battleground for foreign troops.

The Queen's ministers begged her to execute Mary. Time after time, they produced proof of plots to overthrow the government, to kill the Queen and restore the Roman Catholic religion, but Elizabeth hesitated. Mary was her cousin; she was a queen and, in a sense, a guest. Perhaps the plots were exaggerated, perhaps her cousin knew nothing about them. But the proofs piled up and, at last, Elizabeth signed the death-warrant. Afterwards, she wept bitterly and laid the blame upon her Council.

For Philip, the execution of Mary Queen of Scots was the last straw. Elizabeth had deceived him for thirty years, pretending she was about to change her religion, pretending she was going to marry this prince or that one, pretending she was his true friend, and all the time she had been secretly helping the Protestant Netherlanders and encouraging her pirates to rob his ships. Now she had killed the cousin whom for so long he had meant to place on England's throne. He must put everything else aside in order to destroy this deceitful woman and to bring her kingdom back to the truth faith.

He assembled the greatest fleet that had ever put to sea. Drake delayed its sailing by a whole year but in July 1588, the Armada entered the English Channel.

Elizabeth's people were ready to defend their island. The Queen had found the money to build some warships and the sea-towns supplied the rest of the fleet that harried the Armada like a swarm of hornets, and finally, with the aid of a storm, broke its majestic power to send the fragments flying northwards to escape the weather and the English guns.

The Queen herself went down to Tilbury on the north bank of the Thames, where Leicester commanded the army that stood ready to oppose the Spanish soldiers if they got ashore. As ever, she rose to the occasion, put on a steel breastplate, mounted a white horse and, with a page carrying her plumed helmet before her, rode into the ranks of her army:

'I am come amongst you, as you see,' she cried, 'to lay down for my God and for my kingdom and for my people, my honour and my blood, even in the dust. I know I have the body of a weak and feeble woman but I have the heart and stomach of a king, and of a king of England too, and think foul scorn that Parma or Spain or any prince of Europe should dare to invade the borders of my realm!'

Parma's soldiers never arrived and Elizabeth did not have to lead her countrymen in defence of their land, but it was the pinnacle of her reign. All Europe was dumbfounded by this extraordinary woman, queen of only half an island, who had defied and defeated the greatest king on earth.

Danger was not ended, for Philip never gave up his dream of conquering England and there was war for many years – at sea, in Ireland and in the Netherlands. But England had grown up.

The last of the Armada

Under such a Queen, the people found confidence in themselves. They had beaten the Spaniards, they could do anything. Their sailors, explorers and merchants went farther afield and brought home greater riches; their poets, writers and scientists suddenly found amazing energy and skill. New ideas, new buildings, better crops, more trade, more beauty, more splendour were to be seen on every side. It was as though, after a long winter, a tree had burst into blossom.

The Queen grew old and her moods more uncertain than ever, though she still delighted in the company of her young men whom she kept so jealously at Court. They wrote poems in her honour and praised her with lavish compliments. It seemed ridiculous that an ageing woman with bad teeth and a red wig should be courted as if she were a beautiful princess, but Elizabeth had the power to inspire the young men who would serve her at sea and on the battlefield to their last breath.

They called her 'Gloriana' and 'the Faery Queen'. 'She is our God on earth,' said one of her ministers and when Drake returned to Plymouth after his three-year voyage round the world, his first question to a passing skiff was, 'Is the Queen alive and in good health?'

What was the secret of her fascination and how did she raise a bankrupt little island to the ranks of the Great Powers?

Elizabeth was an actress in an age that loved a show. She looked a queen and dressed like a queen. On her Progresses, those summertime journeys about the country, she travelled like an empress, with 300 waggons and 2,000 horses, kindling her people's love by her heartiness and acts of royal generosity. The country people flocked to see her pass, as she rode by on horseback or was carried in a litter in the midst of her splendid Court. She was better-known and better-loved than any previous English monarch.

She was vain, but she could do all the things that people admired. She danced and rode superbly; she could kill a running deer with a shot from her bow and she hunted until she was nearly seventy. As a musician, she was almost as good as her father; as a scholar, she could converse with the university dons and, as she said herself, she could speak six languages better than her own.

Like her father, Elizabeth was royal to her fingertips.

When she was angry, the Court trembled, and when she smiled, the sun shone, but she was neither cruel nor greedy. In one of her tempers, she would swear like a sea-captain, box the ears of her courtiers and, once, she took off a shoe and hurled it at Walsingham. Then suddenly, she would sparkle with fun, calling her ministers and suitors by the nicknames she invented – 'my faithful Moor', 'my monkey', 'my Frog Prince' and 'my little black husband'.

At a solemn ceremony, she could not help tickling the neck of the kneeling Earl of Leicester, and when an ambassador from Poland delivered a threatening message, she rose with a flood of furious insults and turned away in outraged dignity to remark in a loud whisper that it was a pity her favourite Essex was not present to hear how good her Latin still was.

No wonder she never married. All the world, except Elizabeth, thought it impossible for a woman to rule alone, but she kept her princely suitors dangling for thirty years and never intended to share her throne with any of them.

She loved England. She said she had taken England for her husband and wanted no other:

'Nothing, no worldly thing under the sun, is so dear to me as the love and goodwill of my subjects,' were her words to her first Parliament and, when she was not far from death, her last speech was almost the same:

'Though God has raised me high, yet this I count the glory of my crown, that I have reigned with your loves.'

There was one thing she could not do. To name her successor, to think of someone else in her place, was unbearable.

Towards the end, after days and nights in a great chair or lying on piled cushions, her ladies got her finally to bed but she refused food and medicine. Semi-conscious, her mind went over the old perils and she seized a rusty sword that was always kept on her bed and laid about her, slashing and stabbing at the curtains. Then, when she could no longer speak, the Secretary of State dared to breathe the name of James Stuart, and Elizabeth raised her hand to her head to show that the crown should go to the son of the cousin whom she had executed.

In the early hours of the next morning, in her seventieth year, the Great Queen died in her sleep and James VI of Scotland became King of England.

MORE ABOUT ELIZABETH

Elizabeth (1533–1603) was the daughter of Anne Boleyn, Henry VIII's second wife, who was executed before the child was three years old. During her childhood, the princess was often lonely and neglected but she found a kind stepmother in Catherine Parr, the King's sixth and last wife.

When Henry died in 1547, he was succeeded by his 9-year-old son, Edward VI. During the reign, Admiral Seymour was executed for treason on the grounds that he planned to marry Elizabeth and seize power, and, although the girl was innocent, she was kept in semi-captivity.

Edward died in 1553 and Mary Tudor became Queen of England. Like her mother (Catherine of Aragon), Mary was a Roman Catholic; she married Philip II of Spain and hoped to bring England back to the authority of the Pope. Mary and Elizabeth were fond of each other but, since the hopes of the Protestants centred on Elizabeth, she was imprisoned in the Tower for a time. Afterwards, she was closely guarded in various country houses until her half-sister's death in 1558.

Mary Queen of Scots was only 7 days old when she became Queen of Scotland but she was brought up in France where, at 15, she married Francis, son of the French King. She was 9 years younger than Elizabeth and far more beautiful but, although she was charming and tragically unlucky, she lacked her cousin's cool commonsense. She was executed in 1587 and, in dying, she left her claims not to her son James, a Protestant, but to a daughter of Philip II who therefore prepared the Armada in order to take the English crown.

LOUIS THE FOURTEENTH

AT the age of five, Louis XIV became King of France. He was a grave, quiet little boy, whose only playmates were the children of palace servants. 'He laughs rarely in his childish games,' remarked a foreign ambassador, 'and stands for long periods without moving. He knows he is the King and wishes everyone else to know it too.'

Knowing that he was King did not help Louis very much because, although his Spanish mother, the Queen Regent, adored him, she was entirely under the influence of Cardinal Mazarin who was determined to be the real ruler of France. So the boy was kept in the background, surrounded by the Cardinal's spies.

Louis' mother gave him religious instruction every day but he had little other training or education. The Royal Tutor reported that he was so lazy that he could teach him nothing: 'I see no point in reading books,' retorted the young King.

But the lonely boy who hated lessons was naturally charming and polite. An Englishman in Paris saw him riding in a procession, 'like a young Apollo, in a suit so covered with embroidery that one could perceive nothing of the stuff under it; he went almost the whole way with his hat in his hand, saluting the ladies. He seemed a prince of a grave yet sweet countenance'.

While Louis was a boy, there was civil war between the followers of the Queen Regent and some of the great nobles, and the young King suffered the humiliation of being hustled into a coach to escape from Paris, of being peered at and pawed by the mob. When the Royal Family returned, the Parisians insisted on seeing the King to make sure he had not been murdered, and Louis lay in his bed, trembling with rage, while some of the mob burst into his room and stared at him.

He kept silent but he never forgot. All his life he hated Paris, and distrusted the great nobles:

'When I am master,' he said to himself, 'I shall not live in Paris and I shall not allow the nobles to behave like princes with their private armies and fortified towns. There will be no royal uncle and no Mazarin to tell me when I may come and when I must go. I shall be King!'

He had to wait until Mazarin died in 1661. On the next day, Louis announced that he would be his own Prime Minister. He was 22 years old and his reign had really begun.

France was delighted. The people were sick of Mazarin's rule, and all classes gave a joyous welcome to their young King. He was handsome and wonderfully dignified; his marriage to Marie-Therese of Spain brought peace between the two countries and everyone felt that a glorious reign was beginning.

At first, all went well. Colbert, the Minister of Finance, was a brilliant man with many ideas for improving the kingdom; industry was encouraged, trade grew prosperous and colonies were founded overseas; roads and canals were improved, the Army was reorganized and the strength of the Navy was increased from 20 to 200 ships. Though the King still disliked his capital, Paris was cleaned, paved and given a police force.

In all these reforms, Louis showed enthusiasm and ability. He had an excellent memory for detail, and he had entirely thrown off his boyish laziness. Every morning he worked with his ministers and in the afternoon, he met his Council. He also spent an hour or two at Latin or another language, because, he said, 'I find it shameful to be ignorant.' In all his activities – working, building, hunting, dancing, even eating – Louis exhausted his ministers and companions by his tremendous energy.

The evening entertainment at Court began punctually at six o'clock and went on until ten, when the King supped in state and afterwards attended a Ball, a musical concert, the ballet or some magnificent form of amusement until two or three in the morning. Often, he would slip away from the festivities to continue his work, and he kept up this programme year in and year out, for his sense of duty and an iron constitution never allowed him to be tired.

He trusted no-one and meant to keep all power in his own hands: 'Never leave to another anything which you can do yourself', was one of his sayings, but there were problems that even the Grand Monarch could not solve.

The curse of France was unfair taxation. The nobles and the rich Churchmen paid almost no taxes at all; the middle-class paid as little as possible, and the cost of all Louis' schemes, of the Court, the Army and the Navy fell heaviest upon the poorest citizens in the land. Worse, the taxes were collected so dishonestly that barely half the money squeezed from the groaning peasants ever reached the Treasury.

Although Louis XIV is often regarded as a hard-hearted tyrant, he was naturally a generous man who was moved by suffering when it came to his notice.

At a time of famine, he had foreign corn given away to the poor: 'I never spent money to better purpose', he said, and he was constantly making gifts to courtiers who were in difficulties, and to his servants, even remembering to send £100 as a wedding-present to the grand-daughter of his old nurse.

He punished officers who cheated the soldiers and executed an overseer who defrauded the workmen at Versailles but, despite his generosity, Louis did not understand money. He squandered fantastic sums on wars and palaces, without a thought for where the money came from and, although he compelled the nobles to obey him like puppets, he did not use his power to make them improve their estates and care for the downtrodden peasants.

The first years of the King's 'personal rule' were brilliantly successful. He had a number of able ministers besides Colbert, all men of the middle-class who owed everything to his favour and were therefore absolutely loyal. As for the nobles, Louis cut away their power by insisting that they should live permanently at Court under his eye. He never forgot a face and knew every nobleman by sight. If one was absent from the evening ceremony, he would say sharply, 'I do not see him here', and afterwards, the culprit was out of favour, out of the sun. The worst fate of all was to be banished from Court to a distant estate.

To occupy these perfumed courtiers, Louis invented numerous posts that were as useless as they were decorative. At the top, there were the Grand Master of the Household, the Grand Chamberlain, the First Gentleman of the Bedchamber, the Grand Falconer and so on. Hundreds of lesser noblemen held less important positions and their wives and daughters held similar titles in the Queen's Household. As the Royal Family increased, there were more posts of honour in the Dauphin's Household and in the service of the younger princes and princesses.

Thus, the King had endless opportunities to reward those who were obedient, and the nobles of France passed their time in a ceaseless scramble for favour, fluttering about the King and living for the moment when they might be noticed, might catch his eye or actually be spoken to.

In the centre of this glittering Court which included the leading painters, architects, writers and poets of the day, Louis shone like the sun that was his emblem. He wanted glory and where should he find it except in war?

He soon found an excuse to invade the Spanish Netherlands where he captured several frontier towns.

The Powers of Europe were alarmed but Louis soothed their fears by making peace. They did not know that he planned to conquer Holland. Playing the game he loved, the Grand Monarch bought off Charles II of England by a secret treaty, and bribed Sweden and the German princes to keep aloof; then his armies, under a brilliant general named Turenne, attacked Holland and overran its defences. Just in time, the Dutch flooded their countryside to save Amsterdam and the French army was forced to retreat for the time being.

When peace was made in 1678, Louis had gained many towns and duchies, parts of the Rhineland and a new province. True, the cost had been staggering and Turenne was dead, but France – that was to say, Louis XIV – was supreme in Europe.

Naturally, the flatterers gave all the victories to the King, not to his generals. He loved military life, for he revelled in hard exercise and was quite indifferent to discomfort and cold. He would spend ten hours at a time in the saddle, reviewing troops and inspecting positions, and he liked to see to the welfare of his soldiers, to visit their bivouacs and to taste their soup to make sure it was good. But the King was no general. He busied himself so much with petty details that he could not realize the plan of a battle or of a campaign. What he really enjoyed was a siege and there were occasions when his generals would arrange a siege for his benefit instead of getting on with the war.

In later years, Louis tried to command his armies from his desk at Versailles but, by then, his good generals had died and the younger ones were men of lower ability whose chief concern was to please their master at all costs.

However, for the moment, Louis was supreme and it was time to dazzle the world with a monument to his own glory.

From boyhood, the Monarch had loved hunting in the woods round Versailles, where his father had built a hunting-lodge. Here, in a Royal Park of 15,000 acres, in a setting of lawns, ornamental lakes, and woodlands, rose the Palace of Versailles whose extravagance astonished the world. Big enough, with the town that grew up outside the park, to house five thousand courtiers, with servants, tradesmen and hangers-on, the Palace was built to provide a sumptuous background for the Sun-King whose golden emblem blazed on every door.

Never, since the days of the Roman Emperors, had one man been surrounded by such pomp. Beneath painted ceilings, in rooms hung with tapestries and masterpieces, where the priceless furniture was changed according to the season of the year, where silent lackeys in uniforms of blue and silver lit 10,000 candles for an evening's pleasure and where hundreds of the most beautiful women and the most elegant gentlemen in the world loitered and gossiped, the Grand Monarch presided over a perpetual ballet.

The first performance took place every morning. The King's rising, or levée, was a solemn ceremony attended by only the most highly privileged. First, the Royal Family, the loftiest nobles and officials entered the Bedchamber and, as the King rose, his dressing-gown was held ready by the Grand Chamberlain. The Master of the Wardrobe pulled off the King's night-shirt by the right sleeve, the First Valet of the Bedchamber by the left sleeve. The King's brother presented the royal shirt, while the Master of the Wardrobe stood ready to pull on the royal breeches. Meanwhile, double-doors were opened and other courtiers were admitted according to rank, until four separate waves of spectators had been privileged to witness the completion of the King's toilet.

Presently, with equal solemnity, Louis proceeded to Mass in the Chapel where he gazed at the altar and the courtiers gazed at him. The whole day was parcelled out into exact periods of work for the Monarch and of idleness for the courtiers until the evening. Then, with the King's punctual appearance, came the games, the dancing and supper in state to the music of massed violins. The day ended with the ceremony of the King's retirement to bed when the most envied privilege was the right to hold the royal candlestick!

This daily routine would have been ridiculous without the King's matchless dignity. Dressed in a plain brown suit, he moved like a god among the glittering men and women, bowing here, speaking a gracious word there and lifting his hat in a manner that was grandeur itself. It was said that the brims of his hats were always encrusted with grease from his habit of raising his hat at mealtimes when he spoke to a lady. Even kings still used their fingers when eating and, for all its magnificence, the Palace was so cold in winter that soup brought from distant kitchens became congealed grease and wine froze in the glasses. But the King was never cold and no one dared to shiver.

Immensely polite himself, Louis gave new standards of behaviour to European society, for he allowed no brawling or raised voices, and he loved elegance, music and the arts. Yet he was selfish. He had no thought for anyone, only for his pleasures and his dignity, and beneath its brilliant surface, the Court was bored and spiteful. It must be said, however, that the King never shirked any of his duties and, despite his heartless treatment of the Queen, he genuinely loved children. In his old age, his greatest pleasure was to visit Saint Cyr nearby, the school for young ladies founded by Madame de Maintenon, his second wife, who was formerly governess to his children.

If the pomp of Versailles showed the world that Louis was rich and all-powerful, it so alarmed the rest of Europe that a league was formed to oppose his ambitions. When William of Orange, the bitterest enemy of France, became William III of England in 1688, the tide began to turn against the Grand Monarch.

Although the French armies won many land victories, they could not break the resistance of England and Holland and, after nine years, France was so exhausted by the struggle that Louis had to ask for peace.

Only three years later, the half-witted King of Spain died leaving all his possessions to Philip of Anjou, grandson of Louis, who immediately announced that he would support the young man and allow him to accept the Spanish crown. This situation provoked another war

The King had a genuine love of children

between France and the rest of Europe, a war in which English and Dutch sea-power and the military genius of the Duke of Marlborough were too much for France.

The battle of Blenheim destroyed a French army; the battles of Ramillies and Oudenarde wrecked the prestige of Louis and brought his country close to surrender. By 1709, a terrible year of frost and famine, France was bankrupt, its armies beaten and its King forced to sell his gold dinner-service and the silver tables from Versailles.

The allies offered peace if Louis would turn his grandson off the Spanish throne, but, in disaster, the old King showed that he still possessed his dignity: 'If I must fight,' he said, 'I prefer to fight my enemies rather than my grandchildren.'

He made one last appeal to his ragged soldiers and they responded magnificently in defence of the soil of France. News came that Marlborough had lost the favour of Queen Anne and was removed from his command:

'This will do for us all that we desire,' remarked Louis for he sensed that, with Marlborough gone, the war would peter out.

Throughout the disasters, the French King had never lost his majestic calm, but Versailles was sadly changed. The stately routine went on as punctually as ever. The courtiers still promenaded among the statues and fountains, still put on full Court dress for dinner, and schemed to catch the Sun-King's attention. But the sparkle had gone, and the Grand Monarch was an old man who had lost his glory.

His last two years were spent in sorrow for the sufferings of France and for the loss of his son, his grandson and an elder great-grandson who died one after another, leaving an ailing child as heir to the throne.

In the evenings, the King would retire to a private room to join Madame Maintenon, and there they would sit in their armchairs like any other old couple. He was still difficult to manage, but she had turned his mind to religion and he felt more comfortable in her company than with any other human being he had ever known.

In February 1715, the Sun-King held a pageant to show a foreign ambassador that he and France were not finished. He ordered the Court to be as magnificent as in the old days and he himself appeared in gold and black, blazing with jewellery worth £50,000. He held himself as upright as ever but he looked ill and was heard, for the first time in his life, to mention the cold. Yet in July, at the age of seventy-six, he actually hunted again and took a long walk across his favourite estate. Obstinately, he carried out all his usual duties but his leg was hurting him and he began to grow weak.

When he was too ill to leave his room, he ordered his orchestra to play outside the doors during dinner, as though nothing were amiss. Then he said good-bye to his family and his servants, apologizing with his usual courtesy for the trouble he was causing. On September 1st, 1715, he died at Versailles, having been King of France for seventy-two years and three months, the longest reign in European history.

The Sun-King, who had dazzled Europe for more than half a century, gave France the kind of glory that the eighteenth century admired, but it was glory founded upon the people's poverty. Seventy-four years after his death, a hungry mob marched to Versailles and put an end to the monarchy and its splendour.

MORE ABOUT LOUIS

During Louis XIV's immensely long reign (1643–1715), France was the foremost country in Europe, but there was little competition from the other nations. Certainly, Holland became a prosperous sea-faring Power and Sweden was important for a short while, but Spain was declining, Austria and Germany were terribly weakened by religious wars, Prussia had not yet trained a remorseless Army, Russia was only beginning to stir and England was suffering a great many ups and downs.

In the course of Louis' reign, England knew six monarchs and a dictator (Charles I, Cromwell, Charles II, James II, William III, Anne and George I), a Civil War and the bloodless Revolution of 1688. There were wars with Spain, Holland and France, battles in Ireland and Scotland, Jacobite plots and religious unrest. Yet, at the end of the reign, England was stronger and France was weaker than at the beginning.

There were four main reasons why Louis failed to take advantage of his position and abilities: his extravagance, his neglect of trade and sea-power, his persecution of the Huguenots and his ambition. This caused most of Europe to unite against him and the alliance produced, in Marlborough, one of the greatest generals in history.

Louis was succeeded by his great-grandson, Louis XV (1715–1774), who tried to rule in the same manner, but he was lazy, immoral and weak. Wars and misrule increased the misery of the peasants and it was upon Louis XVI that their vengeance fell. The French Revolution broke out in 1789 and, three years later, Louis XVI and his wife, Marie Antoinette, were guillotined.

PETER THE GREAT

THE Kremlin is a vast fortress-palace in the heart of Moscow. Behind its red-brown walls are churches, towers and onion-shaped cupolas, green and gold in the winter sunlight. The gloomy palaces are honeycombed with rooms, passages, and chapels where the Dukes of Muscovy once lived and prayed.

One night, in 1683, the dim corridors rang with screams and the clatter of armed men as the fur-hatted guardsmen of the Streltzy, the Royal Guard, burst into room after room stabbing the occupants and hacking down any who stood in their way. A boy of eleven and his mother fled in terror through the passages and out by a secret doorway into the streets of Moscow to the house of a merchant in the Foreign Quarter. From there, they escaped to a lonely township where they lived in a wooden hut near a lake.

The boy was Peter and his mother, Natalie, was the second wife of the dead Tsar Alexis. After his death, there had been a ferocious struggle between the families of his two wives until Sophia, a daughter of the Tsar, urged the Streltzy Guard to cut the throats of Peter's family so that she could rule as Regent for her idiot brother, Ivan.

Peter never forgot that fearful night, nor the time when he had to fly from his hut and hide all night in the woods clad only in a night-shirt, while Sophia's men searched everywhere to kill him.

The boy grew up wild and savage-tempered. He could not read or write until his mother found a Dutch tutor to give him some lessons, but he preferred working with hammer and chisel. Best of all, he liked the games he invented for a gang of playmates, sons of cooks, grooms and seamen. Along the shore of the lake and aboard a rotting, stranded ship, the boys played battles and sieges in which Peter fought and kicked like a madman, beating his companions with whip or club and hurling them into the shallow water. Then suddenly his mood would change, and the boy, as strong as a young bear, would be all laughter and generosity, rewarding his ragged friends with gifts and with the firework-shows that fascinated him all his life.

At 17, his mother's supporters came and took him back to Moscow where he was set up as joint-Tsar with his idiot half-brother. But Peter was not yet interested in ruling Russia. He left that to others while he spent his days and nights with his boon companions in the Foreign Quarter, still playing crazy games and hooligan jokes. His closest friends were Patrick Gordon, a wild Scot, and Lefort, a Swiss exile with plenty of money. For several years, this trio went everywhere together, fighting, drinking and sailing boats.

When he was twenty-four, Peter decided to stop playing the fool. He would rule as Tsar of All The Russias and make his country great. He was now a giant of a man, six feet six inches tall, with enormous limbs and coarse powerful hands; his face, when not angry, was handsome, with big intelligent eyes and an eager expression. Yet he had the habits of a savage.

His country was as savage as his own character. Hardly anyone in Europe had heard of Russia in the seventeenth century, for the vast country, still known as Muscovy, admitted only a handful of foreigners to trade in furs and tallow. Ruled by the Tsar and the boyars, or nobles, the people lived in misery and fear.

There were no schools, factories, law-courts or Parliament; no navy or worthwhile army, no ports or handsome towns. The nobles were uneducated brutes who treated their wives and children as cruelly as the serfs who toiled on their vast estates. The whole country was sunk in ignorance and superstition.

This was the nation that Peter vowed to make as strong as the countries of the West that his foreign friends described. He had heard enough to know that the secret of power lay in armies and navies. Very well, he would have them both. But Russia had no seaports, except Archangel in the frozen North, for the Turks barred the way to the Black Sea and Sweden ruled all the coasts of the Baltic.

'War is the occupation of kings,' said Peter, and he made a surprise attack on Turkey and managed to capture Azov on the Black Sea. Then, realizing that there was much he did not know about ships, he resolved to go to Europe to find out for himself.

The boyars and the priests were horrified. No Russian ever travelled abroad for it was death to leave the country, except as a pilgrim or diplomat. Peter therefore announced that he would permit a party of nobles to go abroad to find allies for a crusade against Turkey.

In 1697, the Grand Embassy set out, with Lefort as Ambassador-in-Chief, eleven diplomats and numerous pages, valets, musicians and four dwarfs. Also in the party was a sergeant of the guards called Peter Mikhai-

In the Royal Dockyard

lov, in reality the Tsar himself, who hopped in and out of this disguise whenever it suited him.

Travelling through northern Europe, the Embassy came to Holland where Peter worked for five months as a ship's carpenter in the dockyards at Amsterdam. Though he enjoyed himself, living in a little hut near the shipyard, he was disappointed to find that the Dutch built their ships out of age-old skill and knowledge of the sea. He wanted to learn about shipbuilding in a more scientific way, so he decided to go to England whose king, 'Dutch Billy', William III, was ready to welcome him as a possible ally.

To the Tsar's delight, William gave him a splendid new yacht, the *Royal Transport*, and offered him the use of Sayes Court, a beautiful house that belonged to John Evelyn, friend of Sam Pepys. Sayes Court had a famous garden but, from Peter's point of view, its best feature was a private gate into the Royal Dockyard of Deptford. Here he could roam as he pleased, examine vessels and work – an old shipwright said afterwards, 'The Tsar of Muscovy worked with his own hands as hard as any man in the yard.'

He also went about London, visiting the Tower and Windsor Castle, calling upon William III at Kensington Palace where he went in one of the backdoors like a coachman. He went down to Portsmouth and was as excited as a schoolboy to be present at a mock sea-battle. 'I would rather be an admiral in England,' he declared, 'than Tsar of all the Russias.'

The Bishop of Salisbury was sent to tell him about religion and government in England. 'He is,' said the Bishop, 'a man of very hot temper and very brutal in his passion . . . has a larger measure of knowledge than might be expected . . . and seems to be designed by nature rather to be a ship-carpenter than a great prince.'

Peter liked the Bishop but he was less interested in religion than in workshops and factories. He was fascinated by the Royal Observatory, the Woolwich Arsenal where guns were made, and by the Mint. He had coin-making machinery sent back to Russia and also a coffin which was far superior to the Russian way of hollowing an entire oak tree. He loved watches and clocks and found out how to repair them; the streak of cruelty in his nature rejoiced at watching surgeons at work or at acting as dentist to his unfortunate companions.

All the time, the Tsar was enlisting seamen, shipwrights, builders and engineers to go to Russia to work for high wages, and he was also enjoying himself. With his friends, he would go roistering in the taverns or sailing on the Thames. There were mad games at Sayes Court where a fine holly hedge was ruined by wheelbarrow races in which the object was to force the Tsar and his drunken companions through the prickly wall and out the other side!

Indoors, the Muscovites behaved like barbarians. An old servant wrote to Evelyn that the house was full of people who were 'right nasty', but his master had no idea what they were at until after they had gone. The floors were covered with burns, grease and ink; the panelling and tiled stoves were smashed; door-locks and window-catches ripped out, pictures slashed, curtains and bed-linen torn to ribbons; 300 window-panes broken and all the chairs, over fifty in number, gone, probably for firewood. As for the green lawns, the trim gravel walks and flowerbeds, they were ruined beyond repair.

The Grand Embassy left England for Vienna where the Court was horrified by the Tsar's clownish pranks. Then news of a revolt by the Streltzy Guard caused Peter to hurry back to Moscow. Although Patrick Gordon, now a General, had easily put down the mutiny of a few troops, the Tsar dealt out punishment with horrible zest.

He took his revenge for the night when his family was murdered. After torture had wrung every secret from the wretched Guards, hundreds were beheaded in the Red Square, many of them by Peter himself who gloried in the slaughter. Two hundred men were hanged outside Sophia's convent and the rest were sent to die in Siberia. The power of the Streltzy was destroyed and Peter could rule as he pleased with the aid of spies and secret agents.

In this atmosphere of terror, he dealt with the boyars, ordering them to discard their old-fashioned robes, to dress as Europeans and to shave off their shaggy beards, many of which he himself hacked off with brutal relish. The nobles were forced to serve him, to pay taxes and to send their sons to be trained to work for the government. The lazy priests and monks were stripped of their riches and the peasants were dragooned into the army or into battalions for building and draining.

Russia trembled but all were helpless. 'To be near the Tsar is to be near to death', ran a popular saying, for Peter went about with a heavy stick and would thrash anyone, courtier or workman, whose stupidity roused his anger. But those who could stand his savage rage were usually well rewarded for their service.

In 1700, war was declared on Sweden, and after several defeats from the great Charles XII, the Russian generals lured the Swedes into Russia, destroying everything as they went, so that the enemy starved and died of disease. By 1709, Sweden was defeated and Russia had gained a strip of the Baltic sea-coast.

On a piece of marshy ground, Peter built the port of St. Petersburg (now Leningrad), one of the marvels of the world.

He dug the first turf himself and lived in a log hut while around him thousands of serfs, prisoners and convicts built a city where there had been nothing but a desolate swamp. Architects were sent to Holland to study the methods of building on marshy land, the use of

Peter the Great's Palace

stone anywhere else in Russia was forbidden, the nobles were forced to build palaces, and 200,000 men died from exhaustion and fever. It was 'a city built on bones', but in less than ten years, Peter had one of the finest cities and best ports in Europe.

Wars went on throughout most of the reign and, as the years went by, Peter grew ever more tyrannical as he began to fear that the sullen boyars would undo his work when he was gone. For this reason, he killed his own son Alexius, and forced everyone into grovelling obedience.

The only person who could control him at all was his second wife Catherine, formerly a servant-girl and camp-follower of the army. She was fat, dirty and dishonest; she loved drink and the barbaric jewellery with which she decked herself from head to foot. But Peter loved her for her cheerful unshockable character. He made her Empress, allowed her to cook his food and wash his clothes and, after his death, she ruled Russia for a time almost as brutally as he.

Was Peter the Great mad? His experiences as a boy left him with terrors and a love of cruelty that could never be put to rest. The Courts of Vienna and Paris certainly regarded him as an insane gorilla and he undoubtedly suffered from fits; his face constantly twitched and his great body often seemed uncontrollable. There were days when he stayed sunk in hopeless gloom, filthy and unkempt, then, suddenly, he would emerge magnificently dressed, filled with energy and gaiety. He cared nothing for human life, murdering countless people by his orders and with his own hands. He was a monster and all Russia sighed with relief when he died at the age of fifty-one. Yet he is called Peter the Great.

By superhuman will, he made Russia into a modern Power. He built an army and his beloved navy, factories and industries to supply them, a government system to support them.

He reformed the Church, the coinage, the alphabet, the calendar. He built a capital in a swamp, gave Russia a coastline, founded schools, hospitals, museums and even a newspaper.

He could not give his people justice, goodness or dignity, for he understood none of those things. But what might he have done for Russia and the world if he had been brought up with kindness and educated with goodwill?

MORE ABOUT PETER

Peter the Great (1672–1725) succeeded in making Russia into a European Power. His reforms were brutal and rapid, but most of them lasted, although the nobles hated progress and the peasants became worse-, rather than better-off.

Peter left a line of rulers, most of them women who were generally healthier than the male members of the Romanov family in which there was such a marked streak of insanity. Peter's second wife became the Empress Catherine I for a short while and she was followed by his grandson, the weakling, Peter II, who reigned from 1727 to 1730. Next came Peter the Great's niece, the Empress Anne and then his daughter, the Empress Elizabeth (1741–1762). She chose a German princess to be the wife of her nephew who, as Peter III, was soon assassinated by the friends of his wife who became the famous Empress, Catherine the Great. Thus, it was a German woman and not one of his own descendants who was destined to carry on the work of Peter the Great.

NAPOLEON BONAPARTE

ON 15th August, 1769, in the Corsican town of Ajaccio, a second son was born to Marie, wife of Charles Bonaparte, a lawyer of Italian descent whose family had lived in Corsica for more than 200 years.

The boy was christened Napoleon, and when he was nine years old, his father sent him away to France to a military school at Brienne. At 16, young Bonaparte entered the French army as a sub-lieutenant in the artillery. He was poor and unhappy, but he worked hard at his profession and studied during the evenings when most young officers were enjoying themselves.

At school, the young Corsican had been unpopular. He was very small, only five feet two inches tall, and his olive-skin and strong accent marked his Italian origin, so that he felt a foreigner among the sons of French gentlemen. But in his work, they had to admit that the sullen Corsican was outstanding, and there was a kind of brooding ferocity about him that prevented them from tormenting him.

When the French Revolution broke out in 1789, Bonaparte remained in the Army for he sympathized with those who believed in liberty and justice, but he soon came to hate the rule of the mob and their utterly unscrupulous leaders.

The violent events in France and the execution of the King and Queen brought about war with several European countries, including England and Austria. The year 1793 found Captain Bonaparte in the Revolutionary force outside Toulon, which was held by French Royalists with the aid of British warships. Bonaparte placed his guns with such skill that the town was captured and the British ships had to withdraw.

He had made his mark and was rewarded with promotion to the rank of brigadier.

Young Bonaparte went to Paris where he found the government in confusion while a cut-throat struggle for power was being waged by the politicians. In this dangerous atmosphere, Bonaparte himself was struck off the list of officers and put into prison for a short time, but luckily he had won the notice of Carnot, the War Minister, and of Barras, a rascally politician.

The Parisians were preparing to overturn the corrupt government when Barras remembered the pale young officer who had captured Toulon.

'I have the very man we need,' he told the frightened Members of the Assembly, though they were hardly impressed when they saw a puny youngster in a threadbare uniform.

Once again, Bonaparte seized his opportunity. He placed field-guns where they could command the bridges and rake the streets leading to the Tuileries Palace where the Assembly was sitting and, at the decisive moment, he gave the order to fire into the advancing crowds. Having saved the government, he looked for his reward, and Carnot obtained for him command of the French army in Italy. At the age of 26, he was a general.

Settling his affairs in Paris, among them his marriage to Josephine, a beautiful widow, Bonaparte hurried to take up his command. He found his army dispirited, ill-armed and hungry. Their officers resented the arrival of the youthful commander who had been placed above them, though Massena, afterwards one of his most famous marshals, remarked, 'The moment he put on his general's hat he seemed to grow two feet taller.'

Bonaparte addressed the soldiers, telling them that he would lead them to victory and wealth if they showed courage. Then, with lightning speed, he dealt blow after blow upon the Austrian armies that had been holding Northern Italy. He drove the enemy out, forced his own treaty upon them, took up residence in a palace near Milan and conducted affairs without a word to the government in Paris: 'Do you think I triumph in Italy, in order to glorify that pack of lawyers?' he said.

Wagon-loads of treasure were sent back to France and Bonaparte's soldiers were now well-fed and splendidly equipped. They adored him and hailed him as their 'Little Corporal', an affectionate nickname which stuck to him all his life.

The conquering hero returned to Paris where the government was only too anxious to find fresh employment for this terrifying young general. His victories had caused all the enemies of France to retire, except Britain, so it was suggested that he should invade England. Bonaparte had other ideas: 'Europe is too small a field,' he said. 'Fame can only be won in the East.'

To win an Empire and to bar the British route to India, he sailed his army to Egypt, captured Malta on the way and speedily defeated the Mameluke tribesmen at the Battle of the Pyramids. Ten days later, Bonaparte learned that his fleet at Alexandria had been totally destroyed by Admiral Nelson and therefore his army was cut off from France:

'This is the hour when men of superior ability show themselves,' he remarked and began to prepare for a campaign against Turkey.

He won victories but the stubborn defence of Acre denied him a road to the East so he skilfully withdrew to Egypt where serious news awaited him.

The government in France was tottering and all his Italian conquests had been lost to the Austrians. Leaving his army, Bonaparte went aboard a frigate which managed to evade the British warships and to put him ashore on the coast of France.

As the one man who could restore order and deal with the foes who were closing in, Bonaparte swept aside the government and, by the people's vote, he became First Consul, with two other Consuls of no importance to assist him. He was ruler of France.

With superb energy, Bonaparte crossed the Alps and routed the Austrians at Marengo, while General Moreau, in the north, won a victory at Hohenlinden. For the time being, the Allies had had enough, and in 1802 the Peace of Amiens was signed.

Now, at last, Bonaparte could show that he was more than a successful general.

He put France upon her feet and gave her many of the benefits for which the Revolutionaries had fought. Law and order were established, with an efficient system of government that has remained, little changed, until the present day. Trade, agriculture, education and scientific studies were encouraged; religious freedom was permitted, and careers were opened to men of ability whether they were rich or poor.

'I wish to do something both great and useful for Paris,' declared the Consul, and orders were given to pull down slums, to lay out parks and wide streets and to construct handsome buildings and riverside quays.

In addition, the country was given new roads and canals, but the greatest gift to France was the Code Napoléon, a system of laws that established justice and provided the foundation for the laws of many other countries in the world.

In 1802, Bonaparte was only 33. He had no rival, and had just been made Consul for life. With a stable government in France, trade and prosperity were on the mend everywhere. If only he could have devoted the rest of his life to serving his country peacefully, he might have been the greatest figure in history. Clear-sighted, imaginative, fired with enthusiasm and knowledge of his own great ability, he had all the qualities of a born commander; unfortunately, he chose to use them almost entirely for war.

In 1804, the little Corporal became Emperor of the French. Other emperors might go to Rome but he had the Pope brought to France, and at the coronation ceremony, he took the crown from the hands of His Holiness and crowned himself. Then he turned and placed a crown on the head of Josephine. The Court was soon as magnificent as in the days of the Bourbons. Generals became dukes and princes, former republicans became courtiers and barons, their ladies' dresses changed the fashions of Europe and everyone, even his mother, had to address the Emperor as 'Sire'.

Meanwhile, war had broken out again and the 'Army of England' was assembled on the cliffs of Boulogne, but the French fleets could not win command of the Channel for a few vital days. In disgust, Napoleon broke up his camp and was already marching against Prime Minister Pitt's allies, when Nelson's victory at Trafalgar made England safe from invasion.

The master of war was now at his best. He had a superb army and a corps of generals who had made their names under his leadership. At Ulm, the Austrian commander surrendered with 70,000 men and at Austerlitz, in 1805, perhaps the greatest of Napoleon's victories, the joint armies of Russia and Austria were smashed.

This was the victory that killed Pitt, for men said his face never lost 'the Austerlitz look'.

Next, the King of Prussia's army was destroyed in a single day at Jena. The French Emperor entered Berlin as he had entered Vienna. He went on to defeat the Russians and to make peace with the Tsar who was utterly captivated by the charm that Napoleon could turn on as easily as the ferocious brutality with which he subdued anyone who opposed him.

Now, at last, he was astride Europe. He made and unmade kings as he pleased. He oppressed and robbed countries whose simple people had believed that the French came to bring liberty; whereas he declared, 'the states of Europe must be melted in one nation and Paris must be its capital'.

When it came to sharing out crowns, he did not forget his family, as long as they showed proper respect. One brother, Louis, was made King of Holland; another, Jerome, became King of Westphalia; Joseph was placed on the throne of Naples and Sicily and when he was 'promoted' to be King of Spain, Naples was given to a sister who had married Murat, one of his generals. Another of his officers, Bernadotte, ruled in Sweden, and Napoleon himself took the title of King of Italy. Only England, 'perfidious Albion', was beyond the conqueror's reach.

For Napoleon, one victory followed another

Plans were made to bring England to her knees by destroying her trade and all Europe was forbidden to do any business at all with the nation of shopkeepers. Since Portugal was a door through which English goods might enter the continent, a French army was sent to crush that small country and Joseph was given the Spanish crown. But the Spaniards and the Portuguese were obstinate people whose countryside was ideal for guerrilla warfare, even if they could not face the French in battle. With the help of the Duke of Wellington and his British redcoats, they defied the best generals whom Napoleon could send and tied up a quarter of a million of his vet-

erans. The 'Spanish ulcer' drained the strength of the Grand Army.

Once more, Austria raised an army but again Napoleon triumphed at Wagram, a victory that was followed by his divorce from the Empress Josephine who alone loved and understood him. She had not given him a son, so she was put aside for Marie-Louise, daughter of the Austrian Emperor, who bore him a son known as the King of Rome.

Still, Napoleon could not rest, for Tsar Alexander was defying his orders about trading with Britain and in 1812, the greatest army ever assembled in Europe perished in the snow on the way back from Moscow.

This disaster gave fresh heart to the oppressed peoples of Europe and the armies of Russia, Austria, Prussia, of the German states and even of Sweden were assembled against the Corsican tyrant.

Faced with overwhelming numbers, commanding troops that were mostly young and untrained for war, Napoleon was never more brilliant. He defeated the Allies twice and was only beaten at Leipzig because his guns ran out of ammunition. 'If I had had 30,000 rounds, I should today be master of the world,' he wrote afterwards. Retreating into France, he won one action after another, but Blücher and the Allies plodded on and, from Spain, Wellington was driving towards the French border.

France's terrible losses were too much to bear and on 11th April, 1814, Napoleon abdicated, said a sorrowful farewell to the Guard, and left France for the Isle of Elba, amid the curses of the people who had once adored him.

Ten months later, a short figure in a grey overcoat and a cocked hat stepped ashore in the South of France, and the eleven hundred veterans who were with him wept as they formed in ranks once more behind their Emperor. They had no horses yet, so they set out to march to Paris with Napoleon at their head, stick in hand.

The news of his escape flew ahead and all along the route, he was greeted with cries of 'Long live the Emperor!' His old soldiers fell into step with their comrades, for the Bourbon king, Louis XVIII, was already unpopular and France wanted its glory back. Troops were sent to arrest him, but at the sight of their former commander, they rushed to greet him and he entered Paris in triumph.

The glory was short-lived, for the dismayed Allies could not trust the man who had towered over Europe. In June 1815, his hopes were broken on the ridge of Waterloo when the Old Guard made its final charge and was driven back by Wellington's infantry and cut to pieces by Blücher's Prussians.

The Emperor reached Paris but found no more support. He tried in vain to reach America and, in the end, he surrendered to the nation which had fought him for twenty years, for he went aboard H.M.S. *Bellerophon* which sailed to Plymouth.

Though he asked for the hospitality of the British people, the fallen Emperor was taken to the lonely island of St. Helena in the South Atlantic, from which there was no escape. After six years spent in writing his memoirs and quarrelling with the Governor, Napoleon died and was buried on the island. Twenty years later, his body was brought back with great pomp and placed in a magnificent tomb in Paris.

Napoleon was probably the greatest general who ever lived. Unlike Alexander and Caesar, he started with no advantages of birth and made his way by sheer brilliance and the force of his personality. Yet all his conquests brought only disaster to France and at the end, he left his country weaker and smaller than when he mounted the guns at Toulon.

His real gift to France was his system of civil government and laws. As he said himself,

'Waterloo will wipe out the memory of my forty victories, but that which nothing can efface, which will live for ever, is my Civil Code.'

MORE ABOUT NAPOLEON

What happened in Europe after Waterloo? Napoleon, as we know, died in 1821 on St. Helena, but the effects of his extraordinary career did not die.

The rulers of Europe, particularly of Austria, Russia and Prussia, wanted to put things back much as they were before the terrible Corsican overturned so many thrones. Above all, they were determined to stamp out everything that might lead to revolution.

But, in many countries, Napoleon's tyranny had awoken a spirit of patriotism in ordinary men and a desire for liberty. So, for years, there were uprisings and revolutions. Greece and Belgium gained independence, the Germans tried hard to become a united country, the Poles, Italians and Hungarians rebelled against their foreign rulers.

In France, the Allies had put Louis XVIII on the throne, and he was followed, in 1824, by his brother Charles X, who behaved as if the French Revolution had never happened. In 1830, Charles was deposed in favour of Louis-Philippe, 'the Citizen King', who gave his country 18 years of peace.

But kindly old Louis-Philippe brought no glamour to the throne and France was bored. The terrific excitement that arose when Napoleon's body was brought home in 1840 showed that the French had not lost their thirst for 'glory'. There was a revolution in Paris in 1848; Louis-Philippe abdicated and Louis Bonaparte, a penniless nephew of Napoleon, became President of a new Republic. Three years later, he seized complete power and soon afterwards was hailed as Napoleon III, Emperor of the French.

THE PRINCESS VICTORIA

ON the 24th of May, 1819, a baby girl was born in one of the many rooms of a shabby royal residence called Kensington Palace. She was the daughter of the Duke and Duchess of Kent and grandchild of His Majesty King George III, but her arrival caused no excitement and hardly a mention in the newspapers.

At the baby's christening, her father wished her name to be Elizabeth, but the Prince Regent insisted upon Alexandrina, in honour of her godfather, the Tsar of Russia. Her mother's name, Victoria, was added as an afterthought.

The birth of a princess aroused no rejoicing because at this time, the Royal Family was very unpopular. George III, very old, blind and quite mad, was pitied, but his seven sons were universally hated.

'Prinny', the eldest son, still fancied himself as 'the first gentleman in Europe', but his elegance had long since faded and he was now disgustingly fat and disagreeable. His only daughter, the charming Princess Charlotte, had died soon after marrying a German prince called Leopold and, since none of his brothers had produced a single heir, it had seemed likely that the House of Hanover would come to an end.

To prevent such a calamity, two of the royal Dukes looked round for wives and they found them, as usual, among the numerous princesses of Germany.

The lady chosen by the Duke of Kent was a sister of the Prince Leopold already mentioned. She was a widow with two children, a boy Charles and a pretty twelve-year-old daughter named Feodora.

The Duke of Kent was a stiff military man, with dyed hair and enormous debts which he hoped Parliament would pay when he had done his duty by marrying. Parliament, however, was not very generous, so the Duke grumbled and stayed on in Germany until it was known that his wife was expecting a baby.

An heir for the House of Hanover had to be born in England, so the royal couple hurried back as cheaply as possible and were given a suite of rooms in Kensington Palace where little Alexandrina Victoria was born. Soon afterwards, the family travelled down to Sidmouth in Devonshire where it was thought the sea air would be better for the baby's health than the sooty atmosphere of London.

At Sidmouth, the peppery Duke went for a walk one day, got his feet wet, took a chill and died. Six days later, poor old George III died at Windsor and fat Prinny became King George IV. The little princess at Sidmouth was now an important baby, for the King had no children nor had his next brothers, the Duke of York and William, Duke of Clarence.

The Duchess of Kent was fully aware of her daughter's importance, but for the moment, she was in a difficult situation. She had little money and few friends. She could hardly speak a word of English and she was faced with the mountain of her husband's debts and the

The donkey was a present from Uncle York

dislike of the Royal Family. King George made it quite clear that he expected her to take herself and her baby back to Germany.

The Duchess refused to go. She was determined to bring up her daughter as an English princess and if the Royal Family would not help, there was the child's Uncle Leopold, living in Surrey on a large income, who would come to the rescue.

So the Duchess and her small household came back to the rooms at Kensington Palace. She was a stout, cheerful person, fond of chatter and of bright silk dresses, but she was also fussy and tactless and she had a marvellous way of making people dislike her.

The household consisted of the Duchess herself, Feodora and her German governess, Fraulein Lehzen, and Sir John Conroy, who was agent and adviser. There were some female attendants and servants, all of them drilled by the Duchess to form a protective ring about the baby, in order to screen the child from the outside world and from the influence of the Court and her scandalous old uncles.

Princess 'Drina, as she was called at this time, was spoilt. The chubby, flaxen-haired child who reminded everyone of her grandfather, captivated the household with her blue eyes and pretty ways. Feodora and her nurses adored her and she did as she pleased, demanding her own way and screaming with temper when anything was not to her liking. Yet she was warm-hearted and she was always sorry for her naughtiness when the tantrums were over.

In later years, Feodora spoke of this period as 'those years of imprisonment', but, for the moment, little 'Drina was happy enough. She had a donkey, a present from Uncle York, to ride in the lovely grounds about the

Palace; there were elderly aunts and uncles living in the various apartments who petted their tiny niece and took her for walks among the flowers and there were a few, though very few, little girls who came to play and to look at her dolls.

When she was five, the self-willed princess came under the guidance of Fraulein Lehzen who declared 'there never was such a passionate and naughty child'. With her beady eyes, sharp nose and shining black head, the German governess resembled a watchful bird, but, for all her odd habits and plain appearance, Fraulein Lehzen was a remarkable woman.

By instinct, this German clergyman's daughter seemed to know exactly what was needed for bringing up an English princess. She stood no nonsense from the wilful child but, while she was teaching her to be self-controlled, she somehow won Victoria's heart. Mamma was strict and always in a hurry; the child loved her Mamma of course, but Lehzen was the person she talked to, the person who understood her. She became obedient and worked hard at her lessons to please her governess, 'dear Lehzen, the best and truest of friends'.

Under Lehzen's watchful eye, a team of tutors took over Victoria's education. The Dean of Chester was in charge, with another clergyman to teach Latin, a Frenchman to give French lessons and various artists to teach drawing which was one of the princess's best subjects. She also liked music and singing, and when she was given an examination at the age of eleven by two bishops, they reported that her knowledge of Scripture and History was 'remarkable in so young a person'.

Life was not very exciting at Kensington. Feodora went to live in Germany, the time-table and the rules were very strict, the food was plain and lessons lasted a long time. There was no fun and even books had to be serious, for Victoria was not allowed to read stories or a novel until she was almost grown-up.

The Duchess guarded the child so closely that she had no company of her own age and hardly a glimpse of the outside world. She was never left alone for a minute, but had to sleep in her mother's bedroom and go everywhere, even up and downstairs, with an attendant holding her hand.

There were rare outings and visits. Victoria liked to go down to Surrey to see Uncle Leopold who was always kind and full of good advice; there was company there and sometimes cousins came on visits from Germany.

Besides her dolls, Victoria was devoted to the dogs and ponies that constantly appear in the diary which she began to keep. A King Charles spaniel called Dash was her favourite: 'I dressed dear sweet little Dash for the second time after dinner in a scarlet jacket and blue trousers'; and there was Rosy the pony: 'We galloped over a green field; Rosy went at an enormous rate – she literally flew ... I fed dear Rosy who is always so greedy.'

One day, there was the never-to-be-forgotten visit when George IV summoned his niece to Windsor where the child was fascinated by his painted cheeks and old-fashioned wig.

'Give me your little paw!' bellowed the King jovially when she arrived and soon, to Mamma's dismay, she was squeezed into a phaeton between the King and the Duchess of Gloucester and taken for a ride in the Great Park.

They went aboard a barge filled with ladies and gentlemen who were fishing to the strains of a royal band that played from another barge. There were cakes and peaches for tea and music all evening at Royal

Lodge. The King beamed at Victoria. 'Come now,' he said. 'What's your favourite tune? What's it to be, hey?'

Innocently, the tired child replied, 'God Save the King', and the day ended happily for everyone.

At home, things were less comfortable. A deadly feud had developed between Sir John Conroy and Lehzen, in which the Duchess sided with Conroy, and Victoria with her dear governess. The Duchess was furious but she dared not dismiss Lehzen because the King, realizing her worth, had recently made her the Baroness Lehzen.

The child's importance grew. Parliament voted her an income suitable for one so near to the throne; the Duke of York died and then George IV himself. The Duke of Clarence became King William IV, a rolling, burbling, seafaring man whose manners were shocking but whose heart was kind enough. Unfortunately, he loathed the Duchess of Kent even more than his brother George had done.

The Duchess made two decisions. First, Victoria must be told of her position as heir to the throne (which Lehzen did by slipping into her history book a piece of paper showing the Royal family-tree) and, second, she must be taken about to view her future kingdom.

Tours were arranged to the West country, to Wales, the Midlands and the Black Country. Although the Duchess was always there, bursting with self-importance and taking the limelight, it was all a delightful change from the schoolroom. Most of all, Victoria enjoyed sailing in the Solent aboard the King's yacht, though Mamma foolishly insisted that warships and coastal forts should fire royal salutes whenever she herself appeared. The old sailor William IV was very cross about this and he issued a special order forbidding what he called 'all these poppings and bangings'.

But the Duchess continued to annoy her brother-in-law. She had refused to attend his Coronation and now he was convinced that she was deliberately keeping his niece away from the Court. He was very fond of Victoria and gave her a wonderful Ball at James's Palace on her fourteenth birthday when she was led into supper as the guest of honour between the King and Queen Adelaide.

The Duchess took care that she herself arranged the next birthday dance. When Victoria was seventeen, the King was not present at her Ball in Kensington Palace, but two German cousins were there, one named Ernest and the other Albert. The dancing went on until past three o'clock in the morning and, next day, Victoria noted in her diary, 'Albert is extremely handsome'.

The King was not well but he had made up his mind to live until Victoria was eighteen, because that was the age at which she could ascend the throne without having to have her Mamma as Regent. He invited them to Windsor for a banquet, but the Duchess made difficulties about the date he had chosen. This annoyed him and then, happening to call at Kensington, he found that the Duchess had taken over a suite of seventeen rooms directly against his orders.

Boiling with rage, William went back to Windsor where his guests were arriving. He greeted his niece kindly and then turned to the Duchess and loudly rebuked her in front of the company.

Worse followed. At the banquet, the King rose to make a speech and he soon worked himself into a frenzy of temper about the Duchess, whom he constantly referred to as 'a person now near me'.

While the aristocratic guests, the Queen, the princess and the white-faced Duchess sat staring at their plates, the King ranted on about the insults he had had to put up with from his sister-in-law; he would endure them no longer; he would not have his authority questioned; he hoped he might be spared a little longer so that 'that person' would never be Regent. He would not allow this young lady to be kept away from his Court and so on and on and on.

When this record piece of rudeness was over, the poor Duchess left the room without a word and soon departed from Windsor.

Despite her humiliation, the Duchess could afford to wait. The King could not last much longer and when her daughter was Queen, the daughter whom she had reared so carefully, things would be different. They would see! Mamma would be the Queen Mother with power and influence, for Victoria was an obedient girl and there was good Uncle Leopold to advise them. Leopold was now King of the Belgians, but his letters came across the Channel in a never-ending stream. Victoria said nothing.

By this time, Victoria was enjoying herself. She rode, she danced, she took an increasing interest in music. She seemed to be bursting with life and high spirits; at Brighton, an observer remarked, 'a more homely little being you never beheld . . . she blushes and laughs every instant in so natural a way as to disarm everybody'. But one of her ladies also said, 'a vein of iron runs through her most extraordinary character'.

Truthful and affectionate, Victoria kept her innermost thoughts to herself and sometimes her mouth, so pretty when she smiled, took on an obstinate downward curve. No one, except dear Lehzen, suspected that the tiny princess – she was barely five feet two inches and used to sigh, 'everyone grows but me' – was a far stronger character than her tactless Mamma.

At last, her eighteenth birthday arrived and the King, too ill to attend the Court Ball, sent her a grand piano as a present with the offer, not to her mother but to herself, of ten thousand pounds a year. The King was content. He had lived long enough to thwart his sister-in-law, 'that nuisance of a woman', and, within a month, he died at Windsor in the early hours of 20th June, 1837.

The Archbishop of Canterbury and the Lord Chamberlain immediately ordered a carriage and drove to Kensington where they arrived at five o'clock in the morning. Apart from a desire to be first with the news, it is not clear why they insisted on waking the princess at such an hour, but they did so. After they had gained admittance to the Palace, the Duchess was roused and asked to inform her daughter that two visitors wished to speak with her upon a matter of the utmost importance.

With her fair hair loose about her shoulders and a cotton dressing-gown over her nightdress, Victoria went into the room where the gentlemen were waiting, closing the door firmly upon her Mamma. She was, as she wrote in her diary, underlining the word, 'alone'. The Lord Chamberlain knelt, kissed her hand and informed her that she was Queen of England. She took the news calmly and returned to her mother's room to dress.

At breakfast, Baron Stockmar, an earnest friend of Uncle Leopold, arrived with advice on how to carry out her duties. At nine o'clock, Lord Melbourne, the Prime Minister, called to kiss his sovereign's hand and to offer her the declaration which she must read to her first Privy Council. He did this with such polish and fatherly charm that he won Victoria's heart for ever. Then there were letters to write, to Uncle Leopold, to Feodora and to Queen Adelaide. All was done quietly and at half-past eleven, Victoria went downstairs to meet her Council.

The slim short girl took her seat in silence before a gathering of lords, ministers, bishops, generals and two royal uncles. Instead of a shy schoolgirl stumbling over long, unfamiliar words, they beheld a calm young woman who read her speech in a beautifully clear voice.

Then, as they came up one by one to kiss her hand, they were further astonished by her dignity and grace. 'She was perfection,' said one politician and even the hard-bitten old Duke of Wellington declared, 'If she had been my own daughter, I could not have wished that she should do better. Why, she not only filled the chair, she filled the room!'

When the Council was over, Victoria went upstairs to Mamma and Lehzen. To their astonishment, she announced that her first request to them as Queen would be to be left alone for an hour. At the end of the first hour she had ever spent entirely by herself, the Queen gave her second command. Her bed was to be removed from her mother's room and a separate bedroom was to be made ready. Her reign had begun.

It was to be a long reign, the longest in British history. Victoria was to know great happiness and sorrow, for she was to marry her handsome cousin Albert, to have nine children and to lose her husband when she needed him most. Her popularity was to rise, to fall away and to climb again to a peak of loyalty that amounted to reverence. Her country was to grow in power and wealth until she was Sovereign of the greatest Empire in all history and she was to live on into a new century and a changed world.

But on that June day in 1837, Victoria knew nothing of what lay ahead, only that she was Queen and, at long last, triumphantly 'alone'.

MORE ABOUT VICTORIA

Soon after her accession, the young Queen went to live at Buckingham Palace and her mother was gently but firmly put into the background. She was upset, but later she and her daughter became firm friends. Lehzen, too, was out of favour for a while but not for long; she retired to Germany but kept up an affectionate correspondence with her former pupil.

In 1840, the Queen married her cousin Prince Albert. It was a happy marriage for Victoria adored her husband, though she was not a sympathetic mother; she did not understand children and actually disliked her eldest son. Albert was serious and far better educated than his wife who, after a brief struggle, allowed him to advise her and play an increasing part in the country's affairs. But he was never popular and only the Queen appreciated his excellent qualities. When he died suddenly in 1861, the Queen was broken-hearted. She went into deep mourning and withdrew so completely from public life that for some years she was very unpopular.

The influence of Disraeli drew her out of retirement and she became evermore respected by her people until at the Jubilee of 1897, there was the greatest outburst of loyal affection that had ever been known in a country where, for three hundred years, the Royal Family had been generally disliked.

The leading statesmen of the reign were Peel, Palmerston, Gladstone and Disraeli, but it was also a period of greatness in literature, science and industry, when Britain's power was at its peak. Victoria herself played a considerable part in politics, though her ministers often found her very difficult and obstinate. Her portraits and photographs usually give her a rather cross expression but, in fact, she smiled often; she had a beautiful speaking voice and a delightful silvery laugh which, to the end of her life, sounded like a young girl's.

If you have enjoyed this book you may also like these:

THE STORY OF BRITAIN *by R. J. Unstead* each 30p

552 54001 3 Carousel Non-Fiction
552 54002 1
552 54003 X
552 54004 8

A country is forged by its history, the battles and intrigues of by-gone ages laying the foundations of today. From its beginnings as an island to the end of the Second World War, this series is the record of the men and women who played a role in shaping the character of England now. It traces the emergence of England as a nation.

LOOKING AND FINDING *by Geoffrey Grigson* 25p

552 54007 2 Carousel Non-Fiction

You can find sunken treasure, hidden away in some long-forgotten shipwreck, or discover the past through scattered fossils and ancient inscriptions. It depends what you're looking for, how you go about finding it. It depends where you're looking, how you go about getting there. But once the search begins, there's no knowing what you might stumble across.

THE WHITE BADGER *by Gordon Burness* 25p

552 54008 0 Carousel Non-Fiction

A badger was born just outside London, in fact only eighteen miles from the city centre. He was discovered by eleven year old Gary and his older brother Phil, who had arrived one day at the author's doorstep with a request to be taken badger watching. Their first find was unusual, for it wasn't an ordinary badger, it was all-white, an albino badger. Gary called him Snowball, and this is his story.

THE BLACK PEARL *by Scott O'Dell* 20p

552 52008 X Carousel Fiction

The Black Pearl belonged to the old men, with legends and stories to tell to pass the time – or so Ramon Salazar had thought, until he came face to face with the devilfish and the struggle for the pearl began. But Ramon had more than the dangers of the sea to conquer. Others wanted the Great Pearl of Heaven, including the evil Pearler from Seville.

TO VANISHING POINT *by Doreen Norman* 20p

552 52003 9 Carousel Fiction

There was a strange glow in the playground. Leaves were blowing round on the ground, but in a perfect circle. Then Hazel noticed something else, something which, somehow, no one but herself could see. A girl was standing looking at her, a silver girl, from another planet.

HOW AND WHY WONDER BOOK OF PRIMITIVE MAN 25p

552 86517 6

Where did Man come from? Scientists call on many sources and techniques to discover our origin, collecting fossils and excavating remains to determine how the first of our own species lived and survived in his primitive environment. A scientific companion to the Carousel series EVERYDAY LIFE IN PREHISTORIC TIMES.

HAVELOK THE WARRIOR *by Ian Serraillier* 20p

552 52007 1 Carousel Fiction

These are the days when evil men conspire to overthrow the monarchy, greedy for the power and wealth of wearing the crown and ruling the land. The King of Denmark is dead, his son Havelok forced to flee the murderous attempts of Earl Godard by escaping to the shores of England. He grows up to be a great warrior, to recover his kingdom.

MYSTERY FOR ARCHIE *by Robert Bateman* 25p

552 52015 2 Carousel Fiction

When Archie volunteered for camera work on the film his school was making for a competition, he didn't expect any problems. But the camera disappeared before the film was completed and Archie was determined to find out who was trying to sabotage their entry. But time was beginning to run out . . .

Available January 1972

HOW AND WHY WONDER BOOK OF OUR EARTH 20p

552 86513 3

Despite Man's venture into outer space, the Planet Earth is still the home of all known peoples. Our solar system may provide a planet of alternative accommodation, but most of us will continue to live on Earth. We should know as much about our planet home as we can. OUR EARTH explains how it was made and how it is changing all the time. A scientific companion to the Carousel series EVERYDAY LIFE IN PREHISTORIC TIMES.

THE STORY OF MAUDE REED *by Norah Lofts* 25p

552 52010 1 Carousel Fiction

Her grandfather was only a wool merchant and his house was not considered suitable for a young girl of noble blood. Maude was now old enough to be taught the accomplishments of a lady; sewing, music and the art of graceful behaviour. But this was the Fifteenth Century, and her school was to be an old dark castle.

EVERYDAY LIFE IN PREHISTORIC TIMES
by Marjorie and C. H. B. Quennell each 25p

552 54005 6 Carousel Non-Fiction
552 54006 4

This series presents a picture in words of how our forefathers lived in their prehistoric world, moving out of their caves into the earliest settlements; discovering metals; making fires; building and constructing the first organized villages. The EVERYDAY LIFE series follows them, detailing their development into civilization as we know it.

These books are available at bookshops and newsagents. If you have difficulty finding them you can buy them by post from the following address:

TRANSWORLD PUBLISHERS LIMITED,
P.O. Box 11, Falmouth, Cornwall.

Please send with your order a cheque or postal order (not currency) to cover the cost of the book, plus 6p for each book ordered to cover the cost of postage and packing.